Our American Century

★

Time of Transition · The 70s

$\star$

By the Editors of Time-Life Books, Alexandria, Virginia

With a Foreword by Dick Cavett

Contents

★

6   Foreword by Dick Cavett

22   Troubled Times:
1970-1979

34   Shapers of the Cultural Landscape
Eight Who Defined the 70s

50   Our Long National Nightmare
The Fall of Richard Nixon

68   The Bloody End of a Bitter War
America Escapes Vietnam

82   Fame, Fads, and Folly
Looking Good and Having Fun

96   Women on the Move
The Feminist Revolution

110   Mainstream Music Runs Wild
The Splintered Sound of the 70s

130   Dark Side of the Decade
A Litany of Woe

146   America Turns Inward
The Me Decade

156   Celebration of Superstardom
A Decade of Memorable Moments

168   TV's Uneven Revolution
Realism Versus "Jiggle"

176   The Decade of the Director
"A Golden Age of Filmmaking"

186   *Acknowledgments*
Picture Credits

187   *Bibliography*

189   *Index*

Foreword

There were the "Roaring Twenties" and the "Fabulous Fifties," but no such neat phrase encompasses this astonishing decade—unless maybe the "Preposterous Seventies." If a writer crammed even half of its events into an invented decade, he'd be accused of overdoing it.

It was a decade suited to the admonition that just because something happened doesn't make it credible. People don't willingly die en masse from swilling poisoned fruit drink. And they don't hijack airliners and then parachute from them. (The hijackings added another reason to fear flying besides the food.)

Life frequently outdid art. Nixon's excruciating good-bye exceeded anything in *Patton* for sheer psychodrama. And I'd somehow repressed the fact that our vice president, too, was swept away in scandal.

Reviewing the '70s you could easily wonder if the gods were testing us to see how much we could endure. Watergate or Vietnam alone would be plenty for one decade. That shocking picture of our Saigon embassy being evacuated reminds me of what a tumultuous time it was for doing a talk show. (Did my guest Jane Fonda deserve the boos she received for treason, or the cheers for clear-eyed bravery?)

A shot of the great Muhammad Ali recalls the show where he picked me up and squeezed me between himself and Joe Frazier, and my comment: "We look like a giant Oreo cookie." I'd forgotten that within weeks of each other Jimi Hendrix and dear Janis left us and swelled my doleful videotape archive of dead rock stars, laughing and chatting. On *Jeopardy* I could have come up with "Who is Mark Spitz? Bobby Fischer? Billie Jean King?" but would have failed on "Male supremacy tennis star" and "He faked Howard Hughes's memoirs."

Every positive seems to have its negative. We gained Mary Tyler Moore but we lost Elvis. We gained *Annie Hall* but we got legionnaires' disease.

The '70s! Finally, we can only wonder at them. And we can congratulate ourselves. We got through them.

Dick Cavett

Americans and frantic South Vietnamese line up for evacuation from Saigon by chopper as the city falls to Communist forces in April 1975. The tragic exodus ended America's involvement in Vietnam.

Bicentennial fireworks light up the Statue of Liberty on July 4, 1976. Americans everywhere gloried in the nation's 200th birthday with parades, cherry pies, and miles of bunting.

In an ironic event of the bicentennial year, an enraged protester against court-ordered school busing in Boston tries to use the nation's prime symbol of freedom and equality as a weapon against a fellow American.

The worst oil spill in history unfolds as the crippled supertanker Amoco Cadiz spews 220,000 tons of crude oil into the waters off France in 1978. The disaster ruined 130 beaches and the region's sea-based livelihood.

Late-'70s New York glitterati—from left to right, Halston, Bianca Jagger, Andy Warhol, and, behind Warhol, Liza Minnelli—party at the exclusive disco Studio 54.

A father of seven experiences the pain of applying for unemployment benefits in 1975. High inflation and a slow economy ended America's postwar economic boom and threw millions out of work.

*Against a spectacular Pacific Ocean backdrop,
Californians soothe body and spirit alike in
that classic embodiment of the laid-back
lifestyle, the hot tub.*

Astronaut Jack Schmitt heads back toward his lu-
nar rover (below) during the Apollo 17 mission in
1972. Fellow astronaut Gene Cernan accompanied
Schmitt on this last manned visit to the Moon.

Troubled Times:
1970-1979

Americans love a party, and on July 4, 1976, they threw a big one, celebrating the country's 200th birthday in a glorious spectacle of flag-waving, marching bands, and fireworks to end all fireworks. In New York City harbor, a stately flotilla of 212 sailing vessels—"tall ships"—from 34 nations joined the festivities. In the piquantly named Pacific Northwest town of George, Washington, residents baked a cherry pie 60 feet square. Practically every city, town, and hamlet from sea to shining sea joyously complied with President Gerald Ford's injunction to "break out the flag, strike up the band, light up the sky."

The celebration could not have come at a better time. The nation, after a quarter century of vibrant post-World War II prosperity and world prominence, had hit a bad patch. Although the '70s were a time of high energy and enthusiasm for life for many Americans, they also proved to be a time of doubt and of transition.

America's longest war had produced defeat, loss, grief, and bitterly divisive anger. A president and a vice president had resigned in disgrace. Inflation and oil shortages throttled the economy. Amid all this, the Bicentennial provided a welcome reminder: Whatever their problems, Americans belonged to one of the stablest, most prosperous, and freest societies in human history.

Erosion of Trust. During the 1960s the government had lied to the public repeatedly about Vietnam. At the beginning of the '70s President Richard M. Nixon widened the war while pledging to end it. Seeking to destroy Communist sanctuaries in neighboring Cambodia, he sent troops across the border. The incursion set off furious protests on college campuses, resulting in the deaths of four students at Kent State in Ohio and two at Jackson State in Mississippi. It also helped trigger a Cambodian civil war in whose aftermath the victorious Communist faction, the Khmer Rouge, would unleash an insane campaign of genocide, killing nearly a quarter of the country's eight million people.

Despite his periodic escalations of the war, Nixon was committed to pulling American troops out in favor of South Vietnamese forces—a policy

A Timeline of the 70s
1970

On the first Earth Day, *20 million Americans across the nation turn out to raise public awareness of the environment and protest against pollution.*

U.S. troops enter Cambodia *to attack Vietcong bases. President Nixon tells a shocked American public that the incursion will deprive the Communists of sanctuaries.*

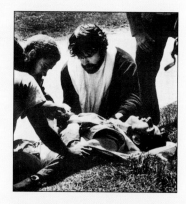

Six students are killed *while protesting the Cambodian incursion—four at Kent State University when fired on by Ohio National Guardsmen, two at Jackson State in Mississippi by police.*

Jimi Hendrix and Janis Joplin, *both 27, two of rock music's most gifted artists, die within weeks of each other from drug-related causes.*

An Arab guerrilla group, *the Popular Front for the Liberation of Palestine, blows up three hijacked airliners—a TWA, a BOAC, and a Swissair—in the desert near Amman, Jordan. The 300 hostages on board are evacuated just minutes before the planes are destroyed.*

"Monday Night Football" *premieres on ABC with play-by-play announcer Keith Jackson and color men Don Meredith and Howard Cosell. The Cleveland Browns beat the New York Jets 31-21 in the inaugural game.*

The Environmental Protection Agency *is created by Congress to establish and enforce environmental standards.*

Black activist Angela Davis, *a University of California philosophy professor, is arrested and charged with kidnapping, murder, and conspiracy in connection with a shootout in a San Rafael, California, courtroom on August 7. She is acquitted of all charges two years later.*

Doonesbury, the comic strip *by Garry Trudeau, makes its debut.*

Vitamin C sales skyrocket *when Nobel Prize winner Linus Pauling asserts that large doses ward off colds and flu.*

New on TV: *"The Flip Wilson Show"; "The Mary Tyler Moore Show"; "The Odd Couple"; "The Partridge Family."*

New products: *daisy wheel printer; quartz wrist watch from Seiko.*

New in print: *Erich Segal's "Love Story"; Richard Bach's "Jonathan Livingston Seagull"; Maya Angelou's "I Know Why the Caged Bird Sings"; "Essence" and "Smithsonian" magazines.*

The Academy Awards: *best picture—"Patton"; best actor—George C. Scott for "Patton"; best actress—Glenda Jackson for "Women in Love."*

1971

Army lieutenant William Calley Jr. *is convicted of premeditated murder for his role in the 1968 massacre of 22 civilians in the South Vietnamese village of My Lai.*

School busing *to achieve racial balance in cases of government-sanctioned segregation is upheld unanimously by the U.S. Supreme Court.*

"All Things Considered," *a late-afternoon news and cultural affairs program, makes its debut on National Public Radio.*

Tricia Nixon weds Edward Cox *in the Rose Garden of the White House.*

The Pentagon Papers, *secret Department of Defense documents about decision making in the Vietnam War, are published by the New York Times.*

he called Vietnamization. In January 1973 a cease-fire agreement with North Vietnamese representatives in Paris enabled the United States to withdraw its remaining forces, ending American involvement after the loss of over 56,000 American lives and a million Vietnamese. American prisoners of war, some of them held in cruel confinement by the North Vietnamese for up to seven years, came home to a joyous welcome.

Vietnamization was more a fig leaf to cover the American pullout than a serious war strategy. Saigon, to the surprise of few, fell to the Communists 27 months after the Paris agreement that Nixon had hailed as "peace with honor." American television viewers watched in horror as South Vietnamese refugees fought desperately to squeeze aboard the last U.S. Marine helicopters leaving Saigon.

The erosion of public trust over Vietnam was made worse by the trauma of Watergate. Nixon had won reelection in 1972 by the largest presidential landslide vote ever. But in pursuit of that victory, employees of his reelection campaign had broken into the Democratic Party's national headquarters at Washington's Watergate complex and pulled off other illegal political shenanigans. Nixon's participation in attempts to cover up these crimes brought him to the brink of impeachment, and he became the first U.S. president ever to resign his office.

Other revelations of government misdeeds further undercut public confidence. The FBI, it was revealed, had spied on thousands of Americans, among them the late Martin Luther King Jr. Congressional hearings uncovered attempts by the Central Intelligence Agency to assassinate unfriendly foreign leaders. A bumper sticker that appeared during the 1976 presidential election campaign summed up the growing cynicism about government and politicians: "Don't vote. It only encourages them."

The Troubled Economy. Even more than the failed war and the abuses of public trust, it was the sudden deterioration of the economy that fostered public discontent. After the two most prosperous decades in U.S. history, the '70s brought double-digit inflation spurred by spending on the war and government social programs, high unemployment, three recessions, and an energy crisis. Interest rates soared as high as 20 percent, and consumer purchasing power shrank so alarmingly that by the end of the decade a 1970 dollar was worth only 43.4 cents.

In October 1973 the first of the decade's oil shortages struck. Beginning

Eighteen-year-olds get the vote *with the ratification of the 26th Amendment to the Constitution.*

Rock star Jim Morrison, *27, of the Doors, dies in Paris of a heart attack thought to be drug related.*

The Kennedy Center *for the Performing Arts opens in Washington, D.C.*

A thousand prisoners riot *and take hostages at Attica State Correctional Facility in New York State; 10 hostages and 29 prisoners are killed when authorities forcibly retake the prison.*

D. B. Cooper skyjacks *a Northwest Airlines flight, lands to pick up $200,000 in ransom, then parachutes from the airborne plane with the money, never to be heard from again.*

New on TV: *"Columbo"; "All in the Family"; "The Sonny and Cher Comedy Hour"; "Masterpiece Theatre"; "Alias Smith and Jones."*

New products: *the microprocessor computer chip by Intel; soft contact lenses; food processor.*

New in print: *William Peter Blatty's "The Exorcist"; John Updike's "Rabbit Redux"; Herman Wouk's "The Winds of War."*

The Academy Awards: *best picture—"The French Connection"; best actor—Gene Hackman in "The French Connection"; best actress—Jane Fonda for "Klute."*

1972

Richard Nixon meets with Mao Zedong, *Communist Party chairman, during the historic first visit of an American president to the People's Republic of China.*

Clifford Irving pleads guilty *to perpetrating one of publishing's great hoaxes: "The Autobiography of Howard Hughes," which he claimed was based on interviews with the reclusive billionaire. Irving and his wife are convicted of fraud.*

The Equal Rights Amendment *is passed by Congress and sent to the states for ratification. Eventually it fails to be ratified by the necessary two-thirds of the states.*

Alabama governor George Wallace *(shown being comforted by his wife, Cornelia) is shot while campaigning for the Democratic presidential nomination in Laurel, Maryland. He is left permanently paralyzed.*

Nixon becomes the first *U.S. president to visit Moscow. While there he signs treaties limiting antiballistic missiles and certain strategic weapons.*

The Democrats' Watergate office *is burglarized by five men acting on behalf of President Nixon's reelection campaign committee.*

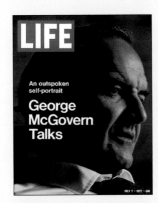

George McGovern is nominated *on the first ballot to be the Democratic candidate for president.*

Jane Fonda, broadcasting from North Vietnam, *urges American soldiers to reconsider their participation in the war, thus earning for herself the demeaning nickname Hanoi Jane.*

Bobby Fischer is the first *American to win the world chess title, beating Soviet grand master Boris Spassky.*

U.S. swimmer Mark Spitz *wins seven gold medals at the Olympic Games in Munich.*

Palestinian terrorists *kill two Israeli coaches at the Olympics and take nine Israeli athletes hostage. The hostages are murdered during a shootout with police.*

"Life" magazine ceases publication *after 36 years. It continues to publish special issues and reappears in 1978 as a monthly.*

New on TV: *"Fat Albert and the Cosby Kids"; "M*A*S*H"; "The Bob Newhart Show"; "Sanford and Son"; "Maude"; "The Waltons."*

with the outbreak of the Yom Kippur War between Israel and its Arab neighbors, much of the oil that flowed to the United States from the Middle East was shut off for five months. Arab members of OPEC—the Organization of Petroleum Exporting Countries—imposed the embargo to punish the United States and other allies of Israel. Americans, accustomed to having all the oil and gas they wanted at a reasonable price, were badly shaken.

The price of crude oil more than tripled. It remained high even after the end of the first embargo because OPEC, feeling its new-found power, kept a lid on production. Practically everything cost more, from home heating oil and gasoline to electricity and plastics. Just to get gas, drivers now had to wait at service stations in lines up to four miles long. To conserve energy, Americans lowered their thermostats, drove smaller and more fuel-efficient cars at reduced speeds, and experienced shortened school and factory hours. Scientists experimented with alternative sources of energy such as solar and wind power and artificial oil from the nation's abundant coal reserves.

In 1971, for the first time in nearly 80 years, the nation imported more than it exported. This imbalance widened through the decade, as Western Europe and Japan became increasingly competitive in electronics, steel, and, especially, automobiles. Consumers turned to German and Japanese cars, which generally were not only more fuel efficient but also better made than Detroit's models. Eventually the federal government had to financially bail out one of the big three automakers, Chrysler, which teetered on the cusp of bankruptcy.

Perhaps for the first time since the Great Depression, many Americans began to question whether their children would have better lives than theirs. As high-paying union jobs in manufacturing disappeared, to be replaced by lesser positions in the growing service industries, the AFL-CIO worried that the United States had become "a nation of hamburger stands, a country stripped of industrial capacity and meaningful work." Book titles such as *Small Is Beautiful* and *The End of Affluence: Limits to Growth* reflected the downsizing of expectations. "Things will get worse," a newspaper headline warned, "before they get worse."

The Quest for Equality. In this climate of political apathy and economic anxiety, the drive for equal rights and social justice lost some of the momentum of the previous decade. Many whites balked when the federal gov-

New products: *Nike running shoes; Home Box Office; Pong, a computer video game from Atari.*

New in print: *"Ms." magazine; Richard Adams's "Watership Down"; Xavier Hollander's "The Happy Hooker."*

The Academy Awards: *best picture—"The Godfather"; best actor—Marlon Brando in "The Godfather"; best actress—Liza Minnelli in "Cabaret."*

1973

The Miami Dolphins *complete an unprecedented perfect 17-0-0 NFL season by beating the Washington Redskins 14-7 in Super Bowl VII.*

The Supreme Court legalizes abortion *without restriction during the first trimester in the landmark Roe v. Wade ruling.*

A Vietnam War cease-fire *is signed in Paris by U.S. national security adviser Henry Kissinger and North Vietnamese negotiator Le Duc Tho.*

Secretariat wins the Triple Crown *with his victory in the Belmont Stakes. He is the first horse to take the Triple Crown in 25 years.*

The last known U.S. prisoners of war *are released by North Vietnam. U.S. troops complete withdrawal from South Vietnam.*

The American Indian Movement, led by Russell Means and Dennis Banks (above), holds out for 71 days against U.S. marshals at the Pine Ridge Oglala Sioux Reservation in South Dakota to protest Indians' living conditions.

Televised hearings on Watergate and its possible White House connection begin.

Billie Jean King beats Bobby Riggs in a "Battle of the Sexes" tennis match in Houston.

Vice President Spiro T. Agnew resigns after pleading no contest to charges of federal income tax evasion. He is succeeded by Congressman Gerald Ford.

Long lines form at gas stations and fuel prices skyrocket when the Organization of Petroleum Exporting Countries (OPEC) cuts off shipments of oil to the United States.

The Saturday Night Massacre causes a national outrage. President Nixon orders the dismissal of Watergate special prosecutor Archibald Cox. The U.S. attorney general and his deputy resign rather than execute the order.

New products: color photocopier; Dungeons and Dragons, a fantasy simulation game.

New on TV: "Kojak"; "Police Story"; "Barnaby Jones"; "The Six Million Dollar Man."

New in print: The Boston Women's Health Book Collective's "Our Bodies, Ourselves"; Peter Maas's "Serpico"; Erica Jong's "Fear of Flying."

The Academy Awards: best picture—"The Sting"; best actor—Jack Lemmon in "Save the Tiger"; best actress—Glenda Jackson in "A Touch of Class."

1974

A nationwide 55-mph speed limit—a measure to reduce gasoline consumption—is enacted as a requirement for receiving federal highway funds.

Muhammad Ali knocks out George Foreman in the eighth round of the "Rumble in the Jungle" in Kinshasa, Zaire.

Newspaper heiress Patty Hearst is kidnapped in Berkeley, California, by a radical militant group, the Symbionese Liberation Army. She is later arrested for joining the group in a bank robbery.

Hank Aaron breaks Babe Ruth's record of 714 career home runs during an Atlanta Braves home game against the L.A. Dodgers.

Mikhail Baryshnikov debuts in the American Ballet Theatre's "Giselle" after defecting to the United States.

Richard M. Nixon resigns the presidency 10 days after impeachment proceedings against him are recommended by the House Judiciary Committee.

ernment, trying to level the playing field in employment, endorsed some forms of the preferential treatment known as affirmative action.

At its best, however, affirmative action meant that able black Americans got a crack at careers from which they had automatically been excluded. Young blacks coming out of college could see the decade of the '70s, for all its troubles, as offering new promise.

White feeling against racial progress was even more pronounced when federal courts, seeking to overcome segregated residential patterns, ordered the busing of students to achieve racial balance in schools. Cities such as Boston and Detroit witnessed the kind of racial violence that northerners had complacently assumed was limited to the South.

Despite racial tensions, a remarkable television production managed to generate unprecedented empathy for black Americans. *Roots,* the 12-hour miniseries based on Alex Haley's best-selling book tracing his ancestors back to West Africa, captivated an audience estimated at 130 million viewers. The most successful miniseries ever, it heightened black pride, white understanding, and a renewed enthusiasm for examining the family tree.

The most influential social movement of the decade affected half of the population directly—and all of it indirectly. Feminism blossomed into a full-blown struggle to challenge traditional male attitudes concerning virtually every aspect of daily life. As the decade progressed, women were able to branch out from their constricted work roles into highly desirable, well-paid careers—anything from corporate CEO to airline pilot to jobs in the skilled construction trades—that formerly had been considered strictly "men's work." For American women the '70s became a time of new-won self-respect and opportunity.

Feminism won perhaps its largest—and certainly most controversial—victory in 1973. In *Roe v. Wade,* the Supreme Court ruled that women had a constitutional right to abortion. The following year, at least one million legal abortions were performed. But the debate over the right or wrong of it was far from settled.

Other protest movements rooted in the '60s rose to prominence. Advocates of gay liberation, taking their cue from the 1969 brawl between homosexuals and police at New York City's Stonewall Inn, emerged to fight for respect and equal protection under the law. Largely as a result of their lobbying, the American Psychiatric Association removed homosexuality from its list of mental disorders in 1973, though

Gerald R. Ford is sworn in *as the 38th president of the United States. He tells the people in his inaugural address, "Our long national nightmare is over."*

President Ford pardons Nixon *for all federal crimes he committed or may have taken part in while in office.*

First Lady Betty Ford *undergoes a radical mastectomy for breast cancer.*

New products: *the pocket calculator; frozen pizzas.*

New on TV: *"Happy Days"; "Chico and the Man"; "Good Times"; "Little House on the Prairie"; "Rhoda"; "The Rockford Files."*

New in print: *Charles Berlitz's "The Bermuda Triangle"; John Le Carré's "Tinker, Tailor, Soldier, Spy"; Alexander Solzhenitsyn's "The Gulag Archipelago"; "People" magazine.*

The Academy Awards: *best picture—"The Godfather, Part II"; best actor—Art Carney in "Harry and Tonto"; best actress—Ellen Burstyn in "Alice Doesn't Live Here Anymore."*

1975

Bill Gates and Paul Allen *start Microsoft, a computer software company, working from an apartment in Albuquerque.*

The U.S. embassy in Saigon *is evacuated by the last Americans. The next day, South Vietnam surrenders to North Vietnam.*

American and Soviet spacecraft *join up. Apollo and Soyuz capsules, in the first cooperative international flight, rendezvous and dock in Earth orbit for two days.*

"A Chorus Line," *a musical about a group of aspiring dancers, opens on Broadway.*

Jimmy Hoffa, former Teamsters' Union *president, disappears in Bloomfield Township, Michigan.*

An assassination attempt *is made against President Ford by Lynette "Squeaky" Fromme, a follower of Charles Manson, in Sacramento, California. Less than three weeks later another attempt is made by 45-year-old Sara Jane Moore in San Francisco.*

In "The Thrilla in Manila," *Muhammad Ali beats Joe Frazier in a 14th-round technical knockout.*

New on TV: *"Baretta"; "The Jeffersons"; "Saturday Night Live"; "One Day at a Time"; "Welcome Back, Kotter"; "Barney Miller."*

New products: *Famous Amos cookies; Wrigley's nonstick chewing gum for denture wearers; disposable razors; the Altair 8800 minicomputer kit.*

New in print: *Harold H. Bloomfield's "TM: Discovering Inner Energy and Overcoming Stress"; James Clavell's "Shogun"; Judith Rossner's "Looking for Mr. Goodbar."*

The Academy Awards: *best picture—"One Flew Over the Cuckoo's Nest"; best actor—Jack Nicholson in "One Flew Over the Cuckoo's Nest"; best actress—Louise Fletcher in "One Flew Over the Cuckoo's Nest."*

1976

Apple Computer Inc. *is formed by Steve Jobs and Steve Wozniak.*

American Dorothy Hamill *wins a gold medal in figure skating at the Winter Olympics in Innsbruck, Austria. U.S. speed skaters Peter Mueller and Sheila Young also take home gold.*

The supersonic airliner Concorde *begins trans-Atlantic passenger service.*

Women are admitted to West Point *for the first time in the academy's 174-year history. The U.S. Naval and Air Force Academies also open their doors to females.*

The black township of Soweto *explodes with the worst racial violence in South Africa's history. Black students, angered by a law requiring the use of Afrikaans, the language of the ruling white minority, are fired on by police during a protest march, resulting in four deaths and sparking the Soweto uprising.*

it redefined the phenomenon as a "sexual orientation disturbance."

Environmental activists grew in number and influence. Their efforts helped bring about the establishment of the federal Environmental Protection Agency and the passage of legislation to safeguard water, the air, and endangered species. Through the efforts of these ecological volunteers, a new concern for the welfare of nature would be firmly established as an American virtue.

The "Me Decade." Despite these movements, the '70s generally saw a retreat from the activism of the '60s toward a search for self-fulfillment and personal happiness. Looking for the good life and fleeing from crowding, crime, and other urban problems, so many people abandoned the cities and headed for the country that, for the first time in this century, rural population actually increased. In the society as a whole preoccupation with self became so pronounced that writer Tom Wolfe labeled the '70s the Me Decade.

This turning inward took surprising forms. Americans tried primal-scream therapy, marathon encounters, Scientology, Gestalt therapy, assertiveness training, transcendental meditation, and sensitivity training. Then there was est—Erhard Seminar Training—the touchy-feely experience dreamed up by an enterprising former encyclopedia salesman who renamed himself Werner Erhard and made millions from his new notion.

Even the pursuit of physical fitness, through jogging, bicycling, swimming, cross-country skiing, and aerobic exercise, contained elements of self-absorption. A book on jogging, of all things, topped the bestseller lists for months, and the "runner's high" ran close competition with the euphoria of drugs. "A good run," said a woman jogger in New York City, "makes you feel sort of holy."

On the other hand, couch potatoes—at least those who combined their indolence with drinking—could take encouragement from the American Heart Association, which announced in 1979 that moderate consumption of alcoholic beverages might guard against death from heart disease.

In their spiritual hunger, many Americans turned to Eastern religions. Some young radicals from the New Left political movement forsook politics and became followers of assorted gurus from India. Other young people flocked to join various cults. Distraught parents hired specialists to extricate their presumably brainwashed children from these groups and

The American Bicentennial *is celebrated in festivities across the country, like the one above in Philadelphia.*

American Legionnaires *meeting in Philadelphia are hit with a mysterious disease; 29 of 180 stricken conventioneers die.*

Romanian gymnast Nadia Comaneci *scores seven perfect 10s and wins three gold medals, a silver, and a bronze at the Olympic Games in Montreal.*

Transsexual Dr. Renee Richards, *formerly Richard Raskind, is barred from competing in the women's tennis competition at the U.S. Open.*

"Treasures of Tutankhamen," a traveling exhibit of artifacts from the young pharaoh's tomb, begins a three-year, seven-city tour of the United States.

British guitarist Peter Frampton's *"Frampton Comes Alive" album is the biggest-selling live pop album ever.*

Two Viking probes, *launched the previous year, begin sending panoramic pictures of the pock-marked, rocky surface of Mars.*

Jimmy Carter is elected *the 39th president over incumbent Gerald Ford with 51 percent of the popular vote.*

New on TV: *"Charlie's Angels"; "The Muppet Show"; "Laverne and Shirley"; "Alice."*

New products: *call waiting; ink-jet printers; Betamax and VHS systems for videocassette recording.*

New in print: *Alex Haley's "Roots"; Ira Levin's "The Boys From Brazil"; Gail Sheehy's "Passages"; Shere Hite's "The Hite Report: A Nationwide Study of Female Sexuality."*

The Academy Awards: *best picture—"Rocky"; best actor—Peter Finch in "Network"; best actress—Faye Dunaway in "Network."*

1977

An unconditional pardon *is granted to virtually all Vietnam-era draft evaders by President Carter.*

A. J. Foyt wins his fourth *Indianapolis 500, the first driver ever to do so.*

The Trans-Alaska Pipeline, *799 miles long, begins oil-pumping operations.*

Elvis Presley, *the "King of Rock and Roll," dies at age 42 from abuse of prescription drugs.*

The National Women's Conference *in Houston draws about 20,000 delegates and observers and drafts a far-reaching legislative program.*

New on TV: *"Three's Company"; "Lou Grant"; "Soap"; "The Love Boat"; "Quincy, M.E."*

New products: *the Apple II computer; magnetic resonance imaging (MRI).*

New in print: *Toni Morrison's "Song of Solomon"; Jim Fixx's "The Complete Book of Running"; Colleen McCullough's "The Thorn Birds."*

The Academy Awards: *best picture—"Annie Hall"; best actor—Richard Dreyfuss in "The Goodbye Girl"; best actress—Diane Keaton for "Annie Hall."*

1978

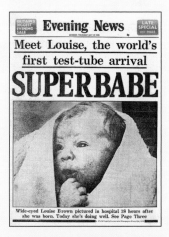

The first test-tube baby, *Louise Brown, is born in England.*

The Love Canal, *a residential area near Niagara Falls, New York, is declared a disaster area by President Carter because of contamination from long-buried toxic wastes.*

Jimmy Connors and Chris Evert *win the men's and women's singles titles at the U.S. Open. Connors beats Bjorn Borg, and Evert beats Pam Shriver.*

"deprogram" them. All cults came under a shadow in 1978 after Jim Jones, founder of the so-called Peoples Temple in San Francisco, led more than 900 followers in a mass suicide at his jungle settlement in Guyana.

A Time to Heal. In the often-neglected public sphere, meanwhile, Richard Nixon's successors attempted to restore the nation's lost faith in government. Gerald Ford, who took office after Nixon's resignation in 1974, was a former Michigan congressman and House minority leader who had been selected by Nixon to be vice president after Spiro Agnew resigned facing criminal indictment. His modest manner—"I am a Ford," he announced, "not a Lincoln"—stirred public confidence. But Ford's inability to tame inflation without plunging the economy into recession, together with his pardon of Nixon, doomed his election chances in 1976.

The new president, James Earl Carter Jr.—a former naval officer, peanut farmer, and Georgia governor who became a born-again Christian—projected a down-to-earth sincerity. In his inaugural parade he chose to walk rather than ride in a limousine. When he addressed the nation on TV about energy shortages, he wore a cardigan sweater to show that the thermostat had been turned down even in the White House. He managed to negotiate a treaty to eventually return the Panama Canal to Panama and mediated the historic Camp David peace accords between Egypt and Israel.

But Carter, too, was bedeviled by inflation, recession, and energy shocks. The revolution in Iran in 1979 interrupted oil supplies, and the other OPEC nations seized the opportunity to hike prices by 50 percent. That summer, consumers lined up in their cars to wait hours to buy gas at an unheard-of price of a dollar a gallon. Then, in November, precisely a year before the next presidential election, came a terrible new humiliation for the United States that Carter seemed helpless to cope with. Iranian Muslim militants seized the U.S. embassy in Tehran and took 65 Americans hostage.

In a nationwide address earlier that summer, Carter had tried to come to terms with the nation's economic and energy woes. With painful candor he spoke of "a crisis of confidence . . . that strikes at the very heart and soul and spirit of our national will." But most of his listeners did not want to hear about an America engulfed in "malaise." Carter would soon be swept out of office by a charismatic former actor radiating the old-fashioned optimism a majority of Americans yearned for after their troubled decade of transition.

Muhammad Ali takes his third *heavyweight boxing title—a record—by defeating Leon Spinks in a unanimous decision in New Orleans.*

The Camp David peace accords *are negotiated by President Carter between Israel's Menachem Begin (left) and Egypt's Anwar el-Sadat (right).*

A mass suicide by poison *is discovered in Guyana, South America. The 912 victims are American followers of cult leader Jim Jones, who is found shot to death among the bodies.*

Tens of thousands of skeletons, *including these near the Cambodian village of Suong, are horrifying evidence of the Communist Khmer Rouge's genocidal policies since assuming power in 1975.*

New on TV: *"The Incredible Hulk"; "Dallas"; "Mork and Mindy"; "Taxi"; "20/20."*

New products: *Epson dot-matrix printer; Harriet Tubman postage stamp.*

New in print: *the "Garfield" comic strip; Herman Tarnower and Samm Sinclair Baker's "The Complete Scarsdale Medical Diet"; Judith Krantz's "Scruples"; James Michener's "Chesapeake."*

The Academy Awards: *best picture—"The Deer Hunter"; best actor—Jon Voight in "Coming Home"; best actress—Jane Fonda in "Coming Home."*

1979

U.S.-Chinese diplomatic relations are established. The United States simultaneously severs diplomatic ties with the Chinese Nationalist government of Taiwan.

The Reverend Jerry Falwell forms the Moral Majority in Lynchburg, Virginia, a right-wing group aiming to reassert traditional religious values in a secular culture.

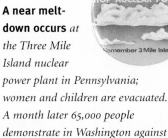

A near melt-down occurs *at the Three Mile Island nuclear power plant in Pennsylvania; women and children are evacuated. A month later 65,000 people demonstrate in Washington against nuclear power.*

Gasoline lines form again *as a 24 percent increase in OPEC oil prices leads to the country's second energy crisis of the decade.*

Skylab falls to Earth. *The 77-ton U.S. space station, launched in 1973, breaks up and comes down in a shower of pieces over the Indian Ocean and Australia.*

Pope John Paul II visits the U.S. *for a seven-day tour beginning in Boston and ending with a farewell mass on the Washington Mall attended by 195,000 people.*

Mother Teresa of India *is awarded the Nobel Peace Prize for her more than 30 years of work among the poor and the sick of Calcutta.*

Iranian students storm *the U.S. embassy in Tehran, taking 65 American hostages. After 13 hostages are released, the rest will remain captive for 444 days.*

Soviet forces invade Afghanistan *following a coup in which the Kabul government of President Amin is ousted.*

New on TV: *"The Dukes of Hazzard"; "Knots Landing"; "B.J. and the Bear"; "Hart to Hart."*

New products: *IBM's 64,000-bit silicon memory chip; the Sony Walkman; the Susan B. Anthony $1 coin.*

New in print: *William Styron's "Sophie's Choice"; Tom Wolfe's "The Right Stuff"; Henry Kissinger's "The White House Years."*

The Academy Awards: *best picture—"Kramer vs. Kramer"; best actor—Dustin Hoffman in "Kramer vs. Kramer"; best actress—Sally Field in "Norma Rae."*

Shapers of the Cultural Landscape

★

What made you a star?" someone once asked television's Johnny Carson. "I started out in a gaseous state, and then I cooled," he deadpanned. But not really. In a
decade sizzling with front-page personalities, Carson was hot. So were comics Richard Pryor
and Woody Allen. In government, Henry Kissinger guided foreign policy with unblinking realism; Jimmy Carter did it idealistically. Gloria Steinem led a social revolution; Jane Fonda spoke
out in many revolutions. And Alex Haley moved the nation with a gripping family tale.

For many of the decade's leading figures, a visit with Carson on *The Tonight Show* was
almost mandatory. Master of the talk-show genre, he drew a vast late-night TV audience.
Carson had begun entertaining as a magician at the age of 14. Rising gradually through radio
and TV, he became NBC's late-night host in 1962. His hallmarks were a boyish personality, a
nimble wit, and a comedic blank stare borrowed from Jack Benny. He made a certain level of
sexual humor acceptable to a mass audience, battling network censors all the way. In one skir-
mish he read nursery rhymes using a censor's "bleep" to create absurd innuendo: "Jack and Jill
went up the hill to BLEEP." "Little Miss Muffet sat on her BLEEP."

A powerful figure in the industry, Carson could launch an entertainer's career into orbit. His private life, though, eluded control. With three failed marriages, he joked, "I resolve
if I ever get hit in the face again with rice, it will be because I insulted a Chinese person."

*Carson was famous for rescuing jokes that bombed. Typical response to audience groans: "This is the type
of crowd that would send an Arrow shirt to General Custer." His career was bombproof.*

Practitioner of Intellectual Power

In 1973 reporters asked Henry Kissinger, PhD, a Harvard professor and the nation's new secretary of state, whether they should address him as Mr. Secretary or Dr. Secretary. "I don't stand on protocol," he said puckishly. "If you will just call me Excellency, it will be O.K."

A flamboyant intellectual born in Germany in 1923, Kissinger served Presidents Nixon and Ford as chief architect of foreign policy in the 1970s. He was a realist who believed that power is paramount in international relations. His secret negotiations produced an arms treaty with the Soviets, new relations with China, a Vietnam peace agreement—which earned him a Nobel Prize—and a measure of peace after the Arab-Israeli Yom Kippur War.

Until marrying Nancy Maginnes in 1974, he had been an unlikely playboy, squiring such Hollywood actresses as Jill St. John and Marlo Thomas. After leaving government, he became a corporate consultant with a base fee of $200,000. Every card in his Rolodex was as good as gold.

A policy that awaits events is likely to become their prisoner.

It would be difficult to imagine two societies less meant to understand each other than the Vietnamese and the American.

Covert action should not be confused with missionary work.

It took me 18 years to achieve total animosity at Harvard. In Washington, I did it in 18 months.

The capacity to admire others is not my most fully developed trait.

Power is the great aphrodisiac.

If history teaches anything it is that there can be no peace without equilibrium and no justice without restraint.

The inscrutable Henry Kissinger, visiting the Great Wall on a trip to China in 1971, was so closemouthed he would not even give reporters his impressions of the scenery.

Family is a mixed blessing. You're glad to have one, but it's also like receiving a life sentence for a crime you didn't commit.

In the world in which I grew up, happiness was a moment rather than a state of being. It buzzed around, just out of reach, like Tinkerbell, flirting and teasing and laughing at your ass.

I made my TV debut on Rudy Vallee's summer variety show On Broadway Tonight. After the show, my family called to congratulate me. My dad, in particular, was tickled. He said, "We're proud of you, son. At least you aren't sticking nobody up."

I'm going to be big. What I'm happy about is I don't owe nobody, and I got enough money to go crazy with. If I have a nervous breakdown, I can be in a private hospital.

By the end of 1970 I just felt full. For the first time in my life, I had a sense of Richard Pryor the person. . . . I knew what I had to do. I had to go back and tell the truth. The truth. People can't always handle it. But I knew that if you tell the truth, it's going to be funny.

With the release of my third album, That Nigger's Crazy, I hit the road. . . . I wish I had a dollar for every person who's told me how they hid that album from their parents and laughed all night when they finally dared play it.

There's nothing better or more exciting than falling in love. . . . However, it's like jumping in a pool when you don't know how to swim. I hear myself screaming, "Edge! Rich, get to the edge!"

Maybe I was just fooling myself by thinking there was more freedom in movies, since I was never going to find an outlet as unrestricted as the stage. Just me, the mike, and the audience.

I like it on top. I got here myself. I earned it. I love it.

A Black Comic's Black Humor

There was a world of junkies and winos, pool hustlers and prostitutes, women and family screaming inside my head, trying to be heard," said Richard Pryor, who grew up in his grandmother's bordello and grandfather's pool hall in Peoria, Illinois. "As a comedian, I couldn't have asked for better material."

Pryor saw his career take off when he stopped trying to imitate the calm cool of Bill Cosby and started listening to those screaming voices from his past. His outrageously funny material, seen on stage and heard on recordings such as 1974's *That Nigger's Crazy,* shocked America with its high-voltage intensity, bluer-than-blue language, and frank sexuality.

Rather than reciting a string of anecdotes and one-liners, Pryor invented full-fledged characters and wove tragicomic stories based on their street-smart wit and wisdom. Playing roles such as Mudbone, an irascible old black preacher, and Lightnin' Bug Johnson, a courtly wino, he demonstrated a talent for character acting that transferred readily to the movie screen.

For his performance as the junkie Piano Man in *Lady Sings the Blues,* a 1972 film about jazz legend Billie Holiday, Pryor received an Oscar nomination. That same year he cowrote the script for Mel Brooks's smash comedy hit *Blazing Saddles* and earned a Writers Guild of America award. In 1974, after crossing over into television, he won an Emmy for a Lily Tomlin special that he cowrote and starred in. At the same time, he continued to put his energy into the comedy stage, winning Grammys in 1975, 1976, and 1977 for recordings of his shows.

Despite these successes, Pryor made TV moguls nervous with his reputation for saying and doing the unpredictable and the outrageous. When he appeared on *Saturday Night Live,* NBC instituted a five-second broadcast delay to "bleep" him, if necessary. His own show, canceled after just four tempestuous weeks in 1977, was overseen by, as he joked, "about 6,000" censors. But, as his friend Bill Cosby said of him, he is nevertheless "a very sane man. That aura of craziness gives his material more impact. It's an intelligent calculation."

Speaking of his many successes, Richard Pryor said, "The biggest moment of my life was when my grandmother was with me on the Mike Douglas Show."

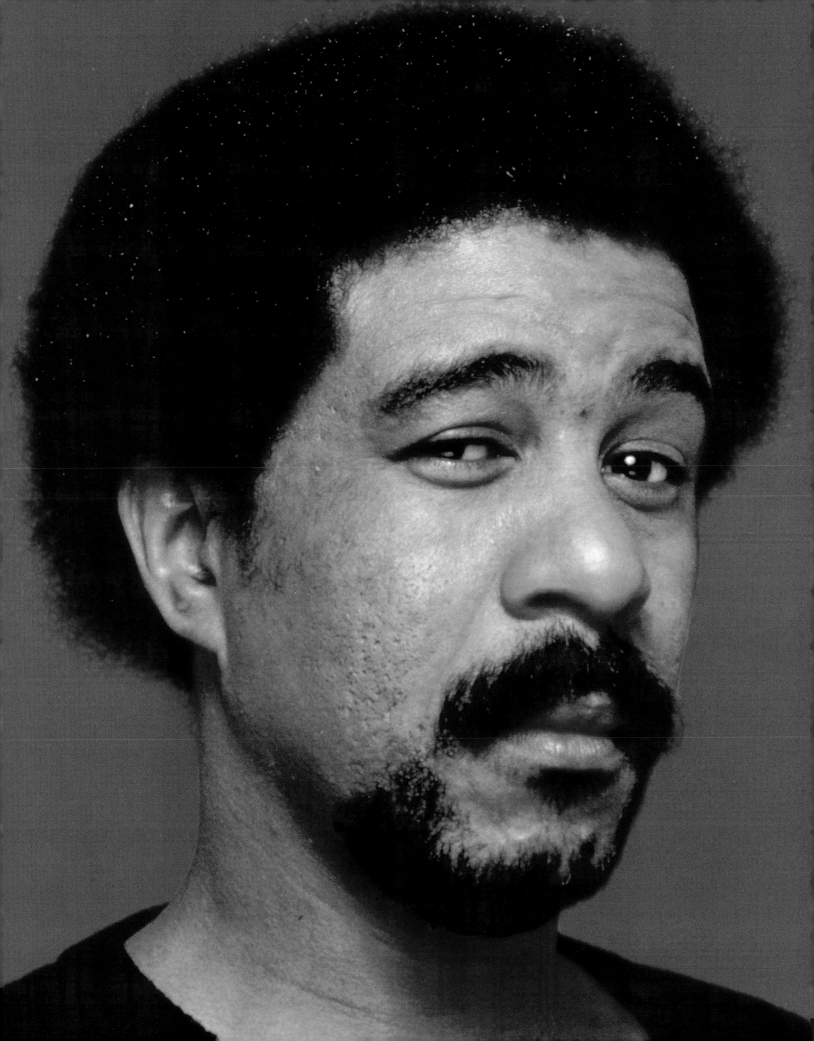

A Constantly Contentious Crusader

Blond ingenue, sex kitten . . . actress Jane Fonda's prior movie roles did little to prepare the American public for the excellence—or the controversy—that would soon attach to her name.

Her performance as a call girl in *Klute* (1971) won her an Oscar for best actress and ecstatic reviews from critics. But her glory was short lived. A few months after collecting her Academy Award she traveled to North Vietnam, where she spoke out against U.S. involvement in the war, denouncing President Nixon as a liar and exhorting American soldiers, "As men, as human beings, can you justify what you are doing?"

Back home, the nation was incensed. Members of Congress wanted Hanoi Jane, as she was quickly dubbed, tried for treason. Ostracized by Hollywood for the next five years, she nonetheless made a triumphant return by the end of the decade, racking up three consecutive Oscar nominations and winning her second statuette for her part in, ironically, *Coming Home*, a movie about a military wife who becomes an antiwar activist.

I was so used to being considered a sex symbol, that I began to like it. I didn't expect people to treat me as a person who thinks.

I attacked my role in Klute like I was doing a research project in college. I went out and watched prostitutes working on the street. . . . It all reinforced my previous feelings about how women, generally, are treated by our system . . . . I remembered my own exploitation as a sex object in the earlier films I had made, and I remembered what the anti-war vets told me about the lives of the vast number of prostitutes in Vietnam—many of them intelligent and trying desperately to get <u>out</u> of the system.

I reached the age of 32 and discovered I'd wasted 32 years of my life. I reached it because of the war, because of the kinds of questions that the Vietnamese struggle is forcing us to ask ourselves about who we are, what our country means, and what we're doing.

I never felt politics touched my life. But, as a revolutionary woman, I'm ready to support all struggles that are radical.

Jane Fonda shows solidarity with welfare-rights demonstrators in 1971. She also championed the causes of farmworkers, Native Americans, and the Black Panthers.

I make any film I want. I don't care if the public likes it, the critics like it. I mean, I would like them to. But if they don't, they don't. I make films for my own enjoyment.

From the time I get up till the time I get to sleep, I think constantly about sex and death.

Money is not everything, but it is better than having one's health.

When we played softball, I'd steal second, then feel guilty and go back.

Most of my characters are so limited locally. They're mostly New Yorkers, kind of upper-class, educated, neurotic. It's almost the only thing that I ever write about, because it's almost the only thing I know.

I've marched with Martin Luther King in Washington. But, when I'm writing, I don't believe in equal opportunity or affirmative action. You can't do that. So when I was trying to draw a picture accurately, it just seemed to me that those families on the Upper West Side almost always had black help. So that's the way I did it. . . . I'm just trying to depict the reality as I experience it, my own authenticity.

I really count Annie Hall as the first step toward maturity in some way in making films.

"Annie Hall" was the first good woman's role I ever wrote.

[I believe in] sex and death. Things which come once in a lifetime. At least after death, you're not nauseous.

I don't believe in an afterlife, although I am bringing a change of underwear.

Not only is there no God, but try getting a plumber on weekends.

The Neurotic as the Ideal 70s Man

Oscar's best picture of 1977, *Annie Hall* marked a turning point in the career of comic genius Woody Allen. Writing, directing, and starring in his own films, Allen had kicked off the decade with comedies such as *Bananas, Everything You Always Wanted to Know About Sex but Were Afraid to Ask,* and *Sleeper*—films that were each, in his estimation, "a series of jokes." But with *Annie Hall* he reached deeper than the belly laugh. He spoke directly to the audience, confession style, about a doomed love affair. He penetrated straight to the heart.

Allen's standard character was the New York nebbish who was likely to say, "My analyst warned me, but you were so beautiful that I got another analyst," or "All literature is a footnote to *Faust.* I have no idea what I mean by that." He was a self-deprecating pseudointellectual, someone who failed at relationships, someone, in Allen's own words, "who is a physical coward, who lusts after women, who is good-hearted but ineffectual and clumsy and nervous." Often obsessed with questions about sex, death, and God, Allen's anguished heroes defined the role of the "sensitive male" that emerged in the 1970s.

As a director, Allen offered more than laughs, a great story, and a profound glimpse or two into the meaning of life. He experimented with lighting, animation, split and wide screens, subtitles, and very long scenes filmed in a single shot. His characters looked into the camera and spoke openly to the audience or were off the screen entirely as they chattered with one another. Even his music was different: In *Sleeper,* his own jazz band—with Allen on clarinet—performed the score. In several other films he simply played old records behind the scenes ("I'm addicted to Cole Porter"). And in *Annie Hall* there was no score at all—only the music heard playing from a car radio or at a party.

Allen claimed that the passion that drove him to produce a new film every year or so came from a single source. "I hate reality," he explained, but added, "Unfortunately it's the only place where you can get a good steak dinner."

"Great humor," said Woody Allen, "is intellectual without trying to be." As a child he had "relatively sophisticated taste in comedy. . . . I never liked clowns."

I'd always understood what made me angry about the Playboy Club or the double standard or being sent out for coffee or not being able to do political writing. But I had thought that my personal problems were my own and not part of a larger political problem.

If you don't want to be a sex object, you have to make yourself unattractive. But I'm not going to walk around in Army boots and cut off my hair.

Progress for women lies in becoming more assertive, more ambitious, more able to deal with conflict. . . . Progress for men will lie in becoming more empathetic, more compassionate, more comfortable working inside the home. . . . We're not trading places. We're just completing ourselves.

The only trouble with sexually liberating women is that there aren't enough sexually liberated men to go around.

Power can be taken, but not given. The process of the taking is empowerment in itself.

We [women] are not more moral, we are only less corrupted by power.

Marriage is something I would consider only out of depression. The surest way to be alone is to get married. Surveys show the happiest people are single women or married men.

At The Ladies' Home Journal where I was an occasional consultant and writer, one of its two top editors (both men, of course) was so convinced that I was nothing like its readers (whom he described as "mental defectives with curlers in their hair") that he used to hand me a manuscript and say, "Pretend you're a woman and read this."

Trying to start a magazine controlled by its female staff in a world accustomed to the authority of men and investment money should be the subject of a musical comedy.

Photogenic Flag Bearer of Women's Liberation

As a glamorous-looking, long-haired, miniskirted journalist, Gloria Steinem was not your typical militant feminist. But she consistently caught the media's attention, and she used the notoriety it gave her in the cause of the sisterhood.

Born in 1934, Steinem grew up with her divorced mother in a rat-infested house in Toledo, Ohio. She escaped on a scholarship to Smith College, where she excelled academically, then headed for New York to be a journalist. Her first published article, a look at the sexual revolution titled "The Moral Disarmament of Betty Coed," appeared in *Esquire* in 1962. She went on to write a hilarious exposé of Playboy Clubs after working undercover as a "bunny," wearing the well-known scanty costume and furry tail. Her story revealed both her sense of humor and her dawning realization of the exploitation of women. She came into her own professionally at *New York* magazine, combining advocacy journalism with political activism.

Steinem embraced feminism after attending a radical women's meeting on abortion laws. "Suddenly," she said, "I was no longer learning intellectually what was wrong. I knew." Having secretly had an abortion herself, she wrote: "If one in three or four adult women shares this experience, why should each of us be made to feel criminal and alone? How much power would we ever have if we had no power over the fate of our own bodies?" Steinem later expressed what she was fighting for in the phrase "reproductive freedom."

Never fitting the media's stereotype of a "women's libber" as an angry, bra-burning radical, she offered instead an expansive definition of feminism: "the equality and full humanity of women and men." In 1971 Steinem helped launch and became editor of *Ms. (pages 102-103)*, a "how-to" magazine "for the liberated female human being—not how to make jelly but how to seize control of your life."

For all her high-profile work on women's issues, Steinem contended that "feminism began (and continues) as a movement of individual women, where they live and work, one by one and in twos and threes."

A tireless political organizer, Gloria Steinem places the name of Frances "Sissy" Farenthold into nomination for vice president at the 1972 Democratic Convention.

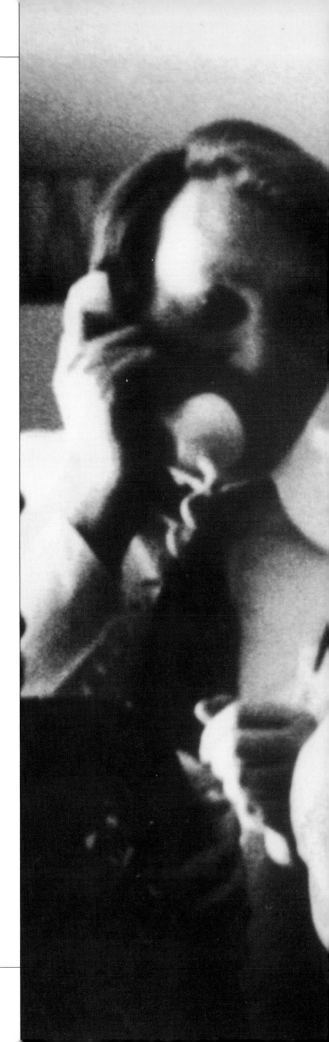

Mr. Carter Goes to Washington

I don't pray to God to let me win an election, I pray to ask God to let me do the right thing," declared born-again Christian candidate Jimmy Carter during the presidential campaign of 1976. Even so, rising as he did from near obscurity as a one-term governor of Georgia, his victory that November appeared to be nothing less than a miracle. Carter's promise of moral leadership seemed exactly what Americans wanted after Watergate had tarnished their faith in government.

Carter reached out to the public. Like ordinary folks, he lowered his thermostat to conserve energy, sent his daughter to public school, and wore blue jeans on weekends.

But in the end he displayed—and advocated for the country—a little more humility than the American people had an appetite for. And he was harmed politically and spiritually by his inability to win the release of the American hostages in Iran *(pages 142-143)*. His greatest legacy may have been that he left office, after a single term, with his principles intact.

I have been accused of being an outsider. I plead guilty. Unfortunately, the vast majority of Americans are also outsiders. . . . The insiders have had their chances and they have not delivered. Their time has run out.

No poor, rural, weak, or black person should ever have to bear the additional burden of being deprived of the opportunity of an education, a job, or simple justice.

My esteem in this country has gone up substantially. It is very nice now [that] when people wave at me they use all their fingers.

Aggression unopposed becomes a contagious disease.

Max Cleland [administrator of veteran affairs] came to tell me goodbye. He brought me a plaque with a quote from Thomas Jefferson: "I have the consolation to reflect that during the period of my administration not a drop of the blood of a single citizen was shed by the sword of war." This is something I shall always cherish.

Jimmy Carter and his wife, Rosalynn, embrace over the news that he has been elected president. Soon afterward, he vowed to "remove some of the trappings" of the office.

The idea that one could roll a blank sheet of paper into a typewriter and write something on it that other people would care to read challenged, intrigued, exhilarated me.

Going to sea is my salvation. It's the one place I know where I can be reasonably isolated and have uninterrupted time to write.

My shipmates . . . asked me to help them write letters to their girls. Pretty soon I was the Cyrano of the ship, composing love letters for all these guys.

History is written by the winners.

Roots is all our stories. It's the same for me or any black. It's just a matter of filling in the blanks—which person, living in which village, going on what ship across the same ocean, slavery, emancipation, the struggle for freedom. . . . The white response is more complicated. But when you start talking about family, about lineage and ancestry, you are talking about every person on earth. We all have it; it's a great equalizer.

There are certain things that a grandmammy or a granddaddy can do for a child that no one else can. It's sort of like stardust—the relationship between grandparents and children. The lack of this for many children has to have a negative impact on society.

The lowest point came during the actual writing. There was exhilaration until I came to the section where Kunta is captured. Then there was dread, anxiety about portraying what he felt when he was chained and during the trip across. I went back to Africa and took a voyage on a freighter, visited the hold, tried to re-create the feeling. . . . I felt a sense of terror, of not being able to capture their feelings. . . . Later I forced myself to go back to the hold. I began to feel the pain, the experience of Kunta. I stayed there all night, in a sense reliving the experience—I felt I was actually in that hold with slaves.

Writing to Prick the Nation's Conscience

When *Roots* aired on TV in 1977, 130 million Americans gathered around their sets to experience Alex Haley's story about seven generations of his family in Africa and America. Much like African villagers gathered around a *griot* storyteller to hear tales of their ancestors, blacks and whites alike were transfixed by the saga that unfolded over eight consecutive nights.

As a boy on his porch in Henning, Tennessee, Haley himself had sat spellbound by his grandmother's stories of their forebears. "Grandmother would bubble with pride about 'Chicken George,' " Haley said, "but when telling about Kunta Kinte, her voice would fill with awe, like she was talking about a Bible story." He would later expand these tales into the bestseller *Roots: The Saga of an American Family.*

Haley joined the U.S. Coast Guard as a young man. Aboard ship, he fought boredom by reading, then by writing. For eight years he pounded out adventure stories on a portable typewriter, receiving hundreds of rejection slips before his first sale.

After his career in the Coast Guard Haley moved to New York City, "prepared to starve," he later recalled, as a freelance writer. He sold stories to *Reader's Digest* and in 1962 initiated the *Playboy* interview series. He collaborated on *The Autobiography of Malcolm X,* a balanced picture of the controversial Black Muslim leader. The book became required reading in colleges and propelled Haley into the big time.

Researching and writing *Roots* took him 12 years. In addition to doing library research, Haley managed to find a West African griot who could still recite the centuries-old saga of his ancestor Kunta Kinte's clan. The resulting book blended fact and fiction, a mix he called "faction."

Awarded a Pulitzer Prize, *Roots* was viewed as a benchmark in U.S. race relations. Affirming the black heritage, it also offered whites a window onto the ugliness of slavery. *Roots* even launched a boom in genealogy. People of all colors and backgrounds seemed to realize, like Haley, that you can't know who you are unless you know where you came from.

Villagers in Juffure, The Gambia, birthplace of Kunta Kinte, joyously greet author Alex Haley in 1977. He had first visited the village while researching Roots.

Our Long National Nightmare

★

THE FALL OF RICHARD NIXON

Down deep he was a loner, rarely comfortable in public. On the hustings he was stiff and awkward, flinging his arms skyward in a well-known pose. He lacked the charisma of the aristocratic John F. Kennedy, who had defeated him in 1960, or the down-home touch of Kennedy's successor, Lyndon Johnson. But by winning the presidency at last in 1968, Richard Milhous Nixon had proved himself to be one of the most resilient politicians in U.S. history.

What powered his comeback were the same cunning, toughness, and persistence that had catapulted this California storekeeper's son nearly to the top early in his career—as conservative Republican congressman and anti-Communist crusader, as senator, as vice president to Dwight D. Eisenhower. Americans had caught a flash of these traits as early as 1952, when he fought for his political life by shamelessly invoking the family dog, Checkers, in a nationwide TV address as Eisenhower considered dumping him from the Republican ticket over accusations of maintaining a political slush fund.

Nixon as president demonstrated a surprising flexibility in domestic affairs. He pursued a centrist, sometimes even liberal path, supporting improved conditions for American Indians, promoting affirmative action in federal hiring, and proposing a Family Assistance Plan to reform welfare and establish a guaranteed annual income for the

Displaying his familiar victory stance, Richard Nixon stands atop a convertible in Chicago's Loop in 1968. It was this campaign that carried him into the White House on his second try.

poor. He presided over the founding of the Environmental Protection Agency and signed legislation to protect health and safety in the workplace.

But foreign policy was his special sphere. Though his quest for "peace with honor" in Vietnam was proving elusive, he did successfully initiate the process of extricating the United States from the Southeast Asian morass *(pages 68-81)*. What's more, this former cold warrior shocked both liberals and conservatives by pursuing accommodation with the two Communist superpowers. With the help of his national security adviser, Henry Kissinger, he moved toward détente with the Soviet Union and achieved a his-

toric breakthrough by opening a dialogue with the People's Republic of China. After journeying to Beijing to meet with Mao Zedong early in 1972, he could announce with pardonable hyperbole, "This was the week that changed the world."

Notwithstanding these triumphs, which helped him earn recognition as *Time*'s Man of the Year for 1971 *(left)*, Nixon remained the loner, isolated in the White House by the force of his nature. He secluded himself behind the "Berlin Wall," the collective nickname for his two top aides, with their Germanic names—Chief of Staff H. R. Haldeman and domestic policy adviser John Ehrlichman.

Haldeman often played the "bad German," taking the heat for the boss's actions—"I'm his buffer and I'm his bastard," he once said. Nixon, however, remained in charge,

In Beijing, ready to plunge into an eight-course banquet and a new relationship with China, Nixon and his wife, Pat, pose with Premier Chou En-lai (on Nixon's right). "I treated them with dignity," he told his cabinet after the historic 1972 visit, "and they treated me with dignity."

Three months after his China sojourn the president schmoozes with Soviet leader Leonid Brezhnev in Moscow. Nixon signed a strategic arms limitation agreement while there, in a climate far more cordial than during his celebrated 1959 "kitchen debate" with Nikita Khrushchev.

not only of major matters but, almost obsessively, of trivial ones. He prescribed the order of seating and serving at state dinners, fretted about whether his Secret Service guards should come to attention or maintain their vigilance during the playing of the national anthem, and once even dictated a memo requesting a wastebasket for the Oval Office washroom.

This passion for control, coupled with a tendency toward political paranoia, led to trouble. In an "us-against-them" White House atmosphere engendered largely by the president himself, aides were motivated to draw up lists of "enemies"—protesters, reporters, entertainers, and others who had angered the administration—and ordered the Internal Revenue Service to harass some of them.

Nixon was so obsessed with secrecy—"almost a basket case," he admitted later—that in his very first year in office 13 aides and four newsmen were subjected to wiretaps because of suspected involvement in information leaks. To gather intelligence on antiwar activists and others, he approved a plan of break-ins, wiretaps, and other illegal activities that, finally, was scuttled only because FBI director J. Edgar Hoover refused to go along, fearing damage to his agency's reputation.

In 1971, after former Defense Department consultant Daniel Ellsberg leaked to newspapers masses of documents—dubbed the Pentagon Papers—detailing the history of U.S. decision making on Vietnam, Nixon made a fateful decision. To plug such leaks, he ordered formation of a special White House investigative unit, nicknamed the Plumbers. Their first action was to burglarize the office of Ellsberg's former psychiatrist in search of information that could be used to discredit him.

The White House's siege mentality and resort to illegal methods spilled over into the 1972 presidential campaign. Despite a growing lead in the polls, Nixon felt he was "in a fight to the death for the big prize." He was determined to employ, as he put it, "the kind of imaginative dirty tricks that our Democratic opponents used against us so effectively in previous campaigns." Plumbers and other operatives forged letters, made phony telephone calls, and distributed scurrilous flyers aimed at smearing or sabotaging Democratic candidates. One such dirty trick contributed to the downfall of Edmund Muskie *(opposite, top)*.

The crowning irony in all the chicanery was how pointless it was. Nixon, to the surprise of no one, overwhelmed George McGovern in one of the greatest presidential landslides ever, gaining nearly 61 percent of the popular vote and carrying 49 states. But now his triumph was tainted: People had been caught breaking the law on behalf of his campaign.

1972 campaign buttons

Comfortably ahead in the polls during the autumn of 1972, Nixon campaigns with uncharacteristic exuberance in Laredo, Texas. One button at left shows Nixon with Vice President Spiro Agnew, who served as his point man in attacks on the Democrats, the media, and others considered to be enemies. Agnew and his speechwriters favored alliterative phrases such as the famous "nattering nabobs of negativism."

Target of a "dirty trick," Senator Edmund Muskie—early front runner for the 1972 Democratic presidential nomination—breaks into tears in Manchester, New Hampshire. A forged letter published in a local newspaper had falsely accused him of using the ethnic slur "Canucks," triggering a scathing editorial against Muskie and his wife. His emotional defense of Mrs. Muskie may have cost him the nomination.

The Botched Break-In That Began Watergate

What came to be known as Watergate began in the wee hours of June 17, 1972, when five men broke into the office of the Democratic National Committee in Washington's Watergate complex. Acting on behalf of the Committee to Re-elect the President (CREEP), the burglars set out to install new listening devices to supplement bugs put in place in an earlier break-in. CREEP wanted to tap the telephone calls of

"I'm not going to comment on a third-rate burglary attempt."

Press Secretary Ron Ziegler, 1972

Lawrence O'Brien, the Democratic national chairman, to gain political intelligence. An alert security guard called the police, who caught the intruders red-handed.

Evidence quickly linked the break-in to CREEP and even to the White House. One of the burglars was James McCord, a former CIA officer who was CREEP's security chief. The two men who supervised the operation from a hotel across the street were "Plumbers" currently on loan to CREEP: E. Howard Hunt, a one-time CIA operative, and G. Gordon Liddy, a former FBI agent. The pair would be indicted along with the five burglars.

The cover-up may have begun as early as June 20, a day after the White House denied any involvement in what it termed a "third-rate burglary attempt." On June 23, for certain, the president ordered the CIA to pressure the FBI to limit its investigation of the break-in, citing national security. He also authorized payment of hush

Except for McCord, all of the Watergate burglars—shown here in police mug shots—had been linked to anti-Castro activity in Florida's Cuban community.

James McCord

Bernard Barker

Eugenio Martinez

Frank Sturgis

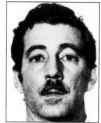
Virgilio Gonzales

Lights blaze in the Watergate office building, scene of the break-in at the ers after a security guard, Frank Wills, noticed tape holding open a lock

U.S. District Court Judge John Sirica upheld his reputation as "Maximum John" in meting out harsh sentences to Watergate burglars.

Below are items of evidence collected by police in the Watergate break-in. These tools of the snoop's trade ranged from the prosaic screwdriver and file to such exotic instruments as the lip-balm container holding a miniaturized microphone for use with a walkie-talkie.

Bag

Wig

Flat file

Rubber gloves

Chap Stick microphone

Screwdriver

Walkie-talkie

Democratic National Committee headquarters. Police arrested the intruders on a stairwell door, removed it, and later found the lock taped open again.

This address book found on one of the Watergate burglars bears the notations "HH" and "WH," with phone numbers. A police tip to the Washington Post about the initials and numbers spurred the newspaper's initial investigation linking E. Howard Hunt, a White House consultant, to the break-in.

Bug Suspect Got Campaign Funds

By Carl Bernstein and Bob Woodward
Washington Post Staff Writers

A $25,000 cashier's check, apparently earmarked for President Nixon's re-election campaign, was deposited in April in a bank account of one of the five men arrested in the break-in at Democratic National Headquarters here June 17.

The check was made out by a Florida bank to Kenneth H. Dahlberg, the President's campaign finance chairman for the Midwest. Dahlberg said last night that in early April he turned the check over to "the treasurer of the Com-

mittee (for the Re-election of the President) or to Maurice Stans himself."

Stans, formerly Secretary of Commerce under Mr. Nixon, is now the finance chief of the President's re-election effort.

Dahlberg said he didn't have "the vaguest idea" how the check got into the bank account of the real estate firm owned by Bernard L. Barker, one of the break-in suspects. Stans could not be reached for comment.

See INCIDENT, A8, Col. 4

Disclosures in the Washington Post such as the one at left, tying the burglars to Nixon's reelection campaign, kept the heat on. Post reporters Carl Bernstein (near right) and Bob Woodward (far right) relied on intensive digging and a secret government source nicknamed Deep Throat to stay ahead of the story.

Author of the plan to bug Democratic headquarters as part of a campaign of illegal activities called Gemstone, former FBI man G. Gordon Liddy co-directed the operation with fellow Plumber Hunt.

White House consultant E. Howard Hunt, Liddy's Watergate partner, was a former CIA operative and spy novelist who tried to live some of his plots.

money to the defendants. Nixon was determined to "stonewall" it, fearing that the truth about Watergate could lead to the exposure of the previous illegalities sanctioned by the White House. "The cover-up is the main ingredient," he said. "That's where we gotta cut our losses."

It almost worked. With the notable exception of reporters such as Carl Bernstein and Bob Woodward *(opposite, bottom right)* of the *Washington Post,* the media for a long time paid scant attention to Watergate. George McGovern tried to make an issue of it during the campaign and failed.

But in March 1973 the White House blanket of deceit began to unravel. For starters, U.S. District Court Judge John J. Sirica, who had presided over the conviction of the burglary defendants, doubted that "all the pertinent facts" had been presented. James McCord confirmed his suspicions.

McCord, who resented Nixon's attempts to shift responsibility for Watergate to the CIA, wrote Sirica a letter asserting that the defendants had been paid to keep silent or to lie. McCord's subsequent revelations sparked a chain reaction. He implicated John Dean, the chief counsel to the president, and Jeb Stuart Magruder, CREEP's deputy director. Magruder, in turn, pointed the finger at others, including the committee's director, John Mitchell, the former attorney general and Nixon's close friend.

Worse, for the White House, Magruder detailed John Dean's involvement. Dean had not initiated the cover-up, but he had orchestrated it and thus knew everything. In early April 1973 Dean began talking to federal prosecutors, and he spread the stain of Watergate to the two men closest to the president—Haldeman and Ehrlichman.

The White House tried to limit the damage by modifying its stonewalling tactics. On April 17, 1973, Press Secretary Ron Ziegler declared that the new information that had come to light rendered all his previous statements about Watergate "inoperative."

Things also unraveled on another front. News broke that L. Patrick Gray, acting FBI director, had destroyed evidence of wrongdoing that Dean had taken from Howard Hunt's office and given to Gray after the break-in.

A few days later, an embattled Nixon went on national television and dropped a bombshell: Haldeman, Ehrlichman, and Dean were resigning because of Watergate, as was Richard Kleindienst, Mitchell's successor as attorney general, who had long been closely associated with the others.

Nixon chose Secretary of Defense Elliot Richardson to replace Kleindienst, and Richardson, eager to restore the integrity of the Justice Department, appointed a Harvard Law professor, Archibald Cox, as a special prosecutor to look into the Watergate affair.

Morality Play for
a Tuned-In Nation

On May 17, 1973, the focus of the Watergate inquiry shifted to the Caucus Room of the Old Senate Office Building. In this marble-columned arena Senator Sam J. Ervin Jr., chairman of the Senate Select Committee on Presidential Campaign Activities, convened the public hearings of what he described as "the most important investigation ever entrusted to the Congress." For the next four months the nation would be mesmerized by this "epic whodunit," as *Time* called it—a daytime TV serial that, for sheer drama, outdid the soaps.

No one was better suited to chair the hearings than Ervin. The 76-year-old North Carolinian was a conservative Democrat, widely respected in both parties for his integrity and knowledge of the Constitution. With his cadenced southern accent and penchant for quoting the Bible and telling homespun stories, he liked to style himself a "country lawyer." But he already had shown his toughness and the rhetorical skills of a shrewd, Harvard-educated attorney in preliminary jousting with the White House. When the president invoked an obscure legal theory, executive privilege, in an attempt to prevent his aides from testifying, Ervin retorted, "Executive poppycock!" The president's men are not "royalty or nobility," he declared, threatening to have them arrested if they failed to appear before the committee.

Ervin became something of a folk hero that summer. With his good humor and unfailing sense of fair play, he seemed to exemplify the search for truth amid the welter of evasive, contradictory, and often confusing testimony. In all, no fewer than 63 burglars, Plumbers, high officials,

Under the glare of TV lights, former White House counsel John Dean takes the oath at the Senate hearings. He testified for five days in a strangely riveting monotone about his role—and Nixon's.

and other witnesses would parade through the Caucus Room, testifying about enemies lists, other break-ins, wiretapping and multi-million-dollar slush funds set up to finance political sabotage and buy the silence of convicted burglars. Some of the witnesses were contrite, others defiant. Many had already told their stories to federal prosecutors. But to Americans riveted to their TV screens most of the revelations were shockingly new.

For the first time, the men closest to the president were compelled to testify in public. John Mitchell, Nixon's former

"What did the president know, and when did he know it?"

Senator Howard Baker, 1973

attorney general and one-time law partner, displayed complete loyalty to the president, despite knowing that two months earlier Nixon had been prepared to offer him up as the Watergate scapegoat. Mitchell said he had not informed the president of such previous "White House horrors" as the Ellsberg psychiatrist burglary: "The most important thing to this country was the re-election of Richard Nixon. And I was not about to countenance anything that would stand in the way of that."

Haldeman and Ehrlichman similarly sought to seal off the president from blame. Ehrlichman labeled the Watergate

A Watergate Lexicon

The Watergate scandal popularized its own vocabulary of words and phrases, such as the following:

Dirty tricks

Inoperative

Stonewalling

Executive privilege

Smoking gun

Expletive deleted

Suffix "-gate" for any scandal

Former attorney general John Mitchell

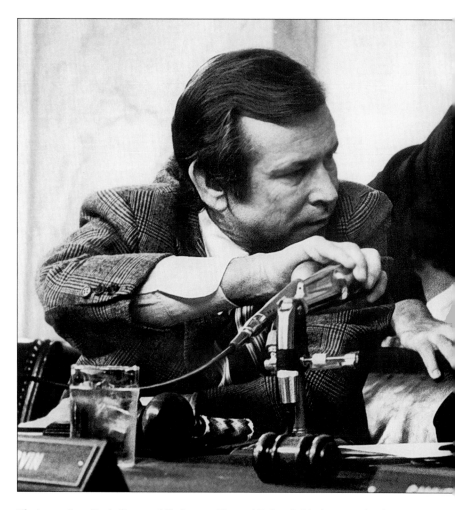

Chairman Sam Ervin listens while Senator Howard Baker (left), the committee's

Former chief of staff H. R. "Bob" Haldeman

Former domestic affairs aide John Ehrlichman

ranking Republican member, confers with Samuel Dash (right), the majority counsel.

break-in "dumb, shocking, irredeemable," but defended previous wiretapping and other transgressions as necessary for national security—"well within the president's inherent constitutional powers," he asserted. Both witnesses attempted to portray John Dean as the real villain in the Watergate cover-up.

Dean proved to be the most compelling—and most damning—witness. Projecting boyish sincerity, he read a 245-page statement and then endured four full days of cross-examination. In contrast to other witnesses, who professed fuzzy memories of dates and events, Dean demonstrated remarkable recall. He recounted his own misdeeds and then accused Nixon of direct involvement in the cover-up. The president, he testified, had talked with him about the possibility of executive clemency and hush money for the burglars. Dean said he had the impression that "the president was well aware of what had been going on."

An even more electrifying revelation followed. Because Dean remarked that he thought one of his Oval Office conversations had been recorded, committee investigators began routinely asking potential witnesses if they had any knowledge of taping. "I was hoping you wouldn't ask that," replied Alexander Butterfield, a former Haldeman aide. Butterfield said that Nixon, to document his role in history, had ordered the Secret Service to install and operate voice-activated tape recorders in the Oval Office, in other presidential venues, and on Nixon's phone. From February 1971 onward all the president's conversations had been recorded.

Fight for the Tapes

"I am not a crook."

Richard Nixon, November 17, 1973

In a televised address to the nation on August 15, 1973—a month after the existence of the tapes was revealed—Nixon (below) again denies taking part in the cover-up.

News of the tapes set off a yearlong effort to pry them out of White House hands. Both Ervin and special prosecutor Archibald Cox subpoenaed them. Nixon refused to give them up. He could have destroyed the tapes, but he felt certain that his argument of executive privilege would prevail in the courts.

Meanwhile, the administration suffered another blow. Vice President Agnew, facing criminal charges of having taken bribes while governor of Maryland, resigned on October 10, 1973. Nixon nominated House Minority Leader Gerald Ford of Michigan to be the new vice president.

Then Judge Sirica and the appellate court ordered the

president to surrender tapes of specific conversations. Nixon proposed providing only written summaries, but Cox refused to accept that, and on Saturday, October 20, Nixon ordered Attorney General Richardson to fire him. Rather than comply Richardson resigned, as did his deputy, William Ruckelshaus. That evening the president finally got Solicitor General Robert Bork to do the deed. This "Saturday Night Massacre" triggered nationwide criticism.

Nixon grudgingly released a few tapes, but on one of them—containing a Nixon-Haldeman conversation recorded three days after the Watergate break-in—a stretch of 18 ½ minutes was erased, further damaging Nixon's credibility.

By the spring of 1974 a new special prosecutor, Leon Jaworski, was breathing down the president's neck, and the House Judiciary Committee was set to start impeachment hearings. Nixon released 1,200 pages of edited tape transcripts. In these documents, with "expletives deleted," as Nixon put it, incriminating dialogue had been expunged, although the vulgar tone of the conversations still shocked the public. Jaworski and the committee refused to settle for them, and the matter went to the Supreme Court.

On July 24 the Court ruled unanimously that executive privilege did not apply to Watergate because the affair was a criminal matter and ordered Nixon to surrender 64 tapes.

Archibald Cox, whose firing by Nixon merited banner headlines, testifies before the House Judiciary Committee on the nomination of his successor. Cox, solicitor general under Kennedy, was succeeded as special prosecutor by a Johnson confidant, Leon Jaworski.

Nixon's secretary, Rose Mary Woods, shows how she "accidentally" erased five minutes from a tape while transcribing it. A panel of experts concluded that 18 ½ minutes of the tape, recorded three days after the break-in, had been deliberately wiped out.

Nightmare's End

During the days after the Supreme Court decision ordering release of the tapes, the emotions of the president vacillated wildly. He went from anguish to fatalistic brooding to shows of bravado. But events were closing in. By July 30 the House Judiciary Committee voted three articles of impeachment, and Nixon could count on little support in the Senate, which would conduct the actual trial. Pressure mounted for him to resign.

Nixon seemed determined to fight on. On August 5, however, the White House, complying with the Court's ruling, made public a tape of a conversation recorded on June 23, 1972, six days after the break-in. It contained what investigators called a "smoking gun." The president could be heard ordering the CIA to block the FBI investigation of the break-in—clear evidence of obstruction of justice.

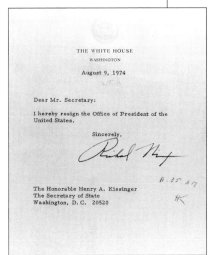

Public revulsion was so overwhelming that Nixon no longer had a choice. Three days later, he told the nation he would resign. He spoke without evident remorse. "I have never been a quitter," he said. "To leave office before my term is completed is opposed to every instinct in my body."

Early the next morning, August 9, 1974, he signed the official letter of resignation *(above)*—the first ever by an American president—and went to the East Room. There, with his family standing behind him *(wife, Pat, at left, and older daughter, Tricia),* he bade an emotional farewell.

Fourteen high officials would be fined or jailed—but not Nixon. He would be pardoned by President Ford, who, after taking the oath of office that historic morning, pronounced an end to "our long national nightmare."

The Bloody End
of a Bitter War

★

AMERICA ESCAPES VIETNAM

When Richard Nixon entered the White House in January 1969, he inherited a nation torn apart by dissent over the Vietnam War. The U.S. military presence in Vietnam had risen to 543,000, and more than 30,000 Americans had been killed. Yet despite endless official predictions of a "light at the end of the tunnel," there was no end in sight. During his reelection campaign Nixon promised to win an honorable peace and "bring the American people together again." Instead, his Machiavellian tactics to extricate the country from the war further polarized the public.

Nixon sought at first to intimidate North Vietnam into resuming negotiations that had reached a stalemate in late 1968. In March 1969 he began a secret 14-month bombing campaign against sanctuaries in Cambodia used by North Vietnam and the South Vietnamese Communist Vietcong guerrillas.

In June Nixon met with South Vietnamese president Nguyen Van Thieu and told him that 25,000 GIs were going home. This withdrawal was the prelude to a major change in military strategy—the gradual turning over of the ground war to the South Vietnamese army and the progressive reduction of the American role *(inset)*.

Within months, the U.S. withdrawal had become policy, euphemistically called Vietnamization, which Nixon announced in a television address in November. He appealed for

---

As the U.S. withdrawal accelerated, troop morale and discipline declined. Many GIs, like these men of the First Cavalry Division in Cambodia in May 1970, ignored uniform regulations—and got away with it.

support to the "great silent majority" of Americans, saying, "North Vietnam cannot defeat or humiliate the United States. Only Americans can do that." The president's popularity temporarily soared, disarming his critics and defusing the effects of massive nationwide antiwar protests held that autumn.

But in April 1970 Nixon lost any goodwill he might have built up when he ordered 20,000 U.S. and South Vietnamese troops into Cambodia to attack the North Vietnamese and Vietcong sanctuaries. Spontaneous protests rocked college campuses. On May 4 at Kent State University in Ohio, jittery National Guard troops fired at a crowd of jeering students, killing two protesters and two passersby. A few days later, two more students were shot by police at Jackson State University in Mississippi.

The senseless shootings prompted nationwide protests. Faculty members and students at more than 400 colleges and universities went on strike. A commission to investigate the unrest, headed by former Pennsylvania governor William Scranton, reported that the rifts in American society were now "as deep as any since the Civil War."

The first major test of Vietnamization came in Febru-

Ohio National Guardsmen aim their weapons at antiwar demonstrators on the Kent State University campus on May 4, 1970 (right). Their fire wounded nine students and killed four, including 20-year-old Jeffrey Glenn Miller (above), who was shot in the head.

ary 1971, when South Vietnamese troops tried to cut the Ho Chi Minh Trail, the enemy's supply line, in neighboring Laos. There would be no supporting American ground troops; a worried Congress had passed legislation forbidding Americans from entering Cambodia or Laos. The venture ended in an ignominious rout of Saigon's forces.

In March, a military court convicted Lieutenant William Calley Jr. of premeditated murder in the killing of Vietnamese civilians at the village of My Lai three years earlier. The events prompted more protests, including one in April by the Vietnam Veterans Against the War *(below, right)*. Public cynicism toward the government's policies deepened in June, when the *New York Times* published the "Pentagon Papers," confidential government memorandums about the war leaked by a former Defense Department consultant *(page 54)*.

On March 30, 1972, the Communists launched an ambitious three-pronged attack. The ensuing five-month-long campaign produced heavy losses on both sides. Nixon responded with stepped-up bombing raids against North Vietnam and the mining of its major ports—sparking fresh waves of outrage at home and criticism abroad.

By now, however, Nixon had succeeded in bringing home more than 400,000 GIs, and peace talks with Hanoi had intensified. Vietnamization, on the other hand, was fooling no one, least of all the North Vietnamese. "How can you expect to prevail with the South Vietnamese army alone," Le Duc Tho, Hanoi's chief negotiator, asked Henry Kissinger, "when it could not win with the assistance of 500,000 Americans?"

A motorized column of GIs clears Route 9 up to the Laotian border in February 1971 in support of Operation Dewey Canyon II, a South Vietnamese effort to cut the Ho Chi Minh Trail in Laos. The exercise failed, exposing the Saigon army's weakness.

Antiwar veterans lift a comrade up the steps of the U.S. Capitol in an April 1971 demonstration. Parodying military jargon, vets named the protest "Dewey Canyon III, a limited incursion into the country of Congress" after U.S.-backed invasions of Laos.

An American Medevac helicopter transports South Vietnamese wounded in Quang Tri Province during the 1972 North Vietnamese offensive. U.S. air power helped blunt the force of the attack.

Forward Air Control pilot Thomas Waskow celebrates completion of his final mission with champagne. "I sure as hell don't want to be the last person shot down," he said before the flight.

GIs returning from Vietnam pass through a gauntlet of peace demonstrators in Seattle. The public's growing revulsion with the war led some civilians to treat Vietnam veterans as pariahs.

The Veterans' Experience

Although nearly three million Americans served in Vietnam, their service and sacrifice went largely unacknowledged by the American public. There were no "welcome home" ceremonies or parades. Instead of returning as whole units with a sense of martial pride, like the men in previous wars, Vietnam veterans were flown back to "the world" alone or in small groups, often straight out of combat with no time for emotional decompression.

"The men who came home from World War II were heroes," explained a Veterans Administration doctor, "but the Vietnam vets were different. The public either felt that they were suckers to have gone, or that they were the kids who lost the war." Many veterans were taunted and made to feel besmirched. "I will never forget flying home and being cursed and spit on and called baby killer by a crowd of kids my age at the airport," a West Point graduate recalled. "I could not believe this was my country."

To add injury to insult, poorly staffed Veterans Administration hospitals were unprepared to treat the thousands of paralytic traumas caused by land mines and booby traps or heal the emotional wounds some had suffered. Instead of adequate care, returning veterans got Hollywood movies and TV shows portraying them as warped. "People think you're a time bomb or an addict," one vet complained.

But the facts belied the stereotype. The vast majority of vets successfully reentered civilian life. A 1977 VA study showed that they earned more money per capita than non-veterans. And according to a Harris survey three years later, 91 percent of the men who had seen combat were "glad they'd served their country."

Earl Robinson, who lost both legs in Vietnam, wears a sad but otherwise inscrutable expression while watching a 1976 Armed Forces Day parade in Chattanooga, Tennessee, with his baby son.

The Quest for Peace

In August 1969 Nixon ordered Henry Kissinger to renew peace talks with Hanoi. Formal meetings, involving the United States, South Vietnam, North Vietnam, and Hanoi's South Vietnamese front organization, the Provisional Revolutionary Government (Vietcong), took place at the Hotel Majestic. Simultaneously, Kissinger and Le Duc Tho, the chief North Vietnamese negotiator, held secret substantive talks in a Paris suburb.

Stalled by mutually unacceptable demands, both sides sought battlefield victories to gain bargaining chips. In the end, a combination of military and political pressures led to a deal. Nixon turned up the heat by ordering a massive bombing of the Hanoi area. At the same time, he was ripe for compromise, being anxious to achieve peace before his upcoming second inauguration. Hanoi, for its part, was eager to see the Americans out of Vietnam, and it had become uncertain of continued support from the Soviet Union and China in light of a recent warming of relations between those two countries and the United States.

On January 27, 1973, the Paris peace agreement was signed. It called for a cease-fire, the return of all prisoners of war, and the withdrawal of American troops within 60 days. The Communists were allowed to hold the areas they controlled in the South pending a political settlement. Vietnam's future was now to be decided by the Vietnamese.

"We have finally achieved peace with honor."

President Richard M. Nixon

Screaming in terror and agony, South Vietnamese children flee down a road after one of their own pilots accidentally dropped napalm on their village in June 1972. The intended target was enemy troops entrenched nearby. The horrifying scene sickened Americans fed up with the seemingly endless haggling at the peace talks.

Flanked by aides, Henry Kissinger studies a line in a document pointed out by his deputy, General Alexander M. Haig Jr., at the Paris talks in November 1972. Shortly before, Kissinger had falsely buoyed American hopes by announcing, "We believe that peace is at hand."

The POWs

Despite all the rancor and divisiveness generated by the war, on one issue Americans found a consensus—everyone demanded the return of the prisoners of war (POWs) and a full accounting of the men missing in action (MIAs). By late 1972, millions of Americans of all political stripes showed their support of this demand by wearing bracelets bearing the name of a POW or an MIA. Officially, the total was 4,383; almost 600 were POWs, mostly fliers shot down over North Vietnam.

Confined in fetid, vermin-infested cells, often in total isolation, the POWs in North Vietnamese captivity suffered grievously. Almost all were brutally tortured to extract information and "confessions." Often their only sustenance was wormy bread and a few bowls of watery soup. The sick and the wounded were left unattended. One air force cap-tain treated his badly burned arm by letting maggots eat away the pus and cleaning the wound with his own urine. The men held by the Vietcong suffered as much or more— they were commonly kept in chains in individual cages.

In Hanoi's infamous Hoa Lo Prison *(below)*, dubbed the Hanoi Hilton by the Americans, conversation between prisoners was forbidden. The POWs developed a secret code that enabled them to communicate with each other by tapping on the thick cinder-block walls of their cells. Only late in the war were they permitted to write an oc-casional brief letter home, like the one at right.

Following the January 1973 peace accord, the POWs were freed in batches, starting with those held the longest. The sight of these long-lost heroes stepping onto American soil, saluting crisply, and embracing their loved ones thrilled the nation. "It's really great to be home," one former POW exclaimed. "In Hanoi we clung to values we believed to be true. They were family, God, and the red, white, and blue."

Air force colonel Robinson Risner leads a group of POWs back to their cells in the "Hanoi Hilton." Risner was a prisoner for seven and a half years.

A letter from a prisoner of war to his wife

"I have been tortured, I have been beaten, I have been placed in solitary confinement. I have been harassed, I have been humiliated."

Commander Richard Stratton, U.S. Navy

The family of Lieutenant Colonel Robert Stirm rush to greet him at Travis Air Force Base in California. He had been a POW for more than five years. The long years of separation caused some couples to grow apart and eventually divorce—including the Stirms.

The Fall of Saigon

For you Americans it is the end," a South Vietnamese remarked after the signing of the peace accord, "but for us it is just another bitter beginning." The prediction was sadly prescient: The only protocols honored were the withdrawal of U.S. troops and the return of the American POWs. Hanoi and Saigon ignored the cease-fire and continued fighting.

In 1973 the South Vietnamese army won back a sizable amount of land, but when North Vietnamese and Vietcong forces counterattacked in the spring of 1974, President Thieu turned again to the United States. Nixon, ensnared in Watergate and curtailed by new laws, could not fulfill his pledge of economic and military aid. Congress was tired of providing what Senator Edward Kennedy called "endless support for an endless war."

The Communists began their final push in January 1975, overrunning province after province. The South Vietnamese army collapsed, its troops joining two million refugees in chaotic flight. On April 30, Saigon fell without a fight. Two weeks earlier, Cambodia had fallen to the Communist Khmer Rouge. Laos, too, would soon succumb to Communist rule. When U.S. helicopters whisked away the last Americans from the embassy rooftop, the nation's tragic and costly Vietnam adventure was finally over.

Fearful South Vietnamese swarm around the walls of the U.S. embassy compound, desperately seeking escape from the advancing Communists.

Fleeing South Vietnamese soldiers atop an armored personnel carrier roar past several dead civilians. During the last months of the war, Saigon's demoralized, poorly led, low-paid army experienced 24,000 desertions a month.

Fame,
Fads, and Folly

★

LOOKING GOOD AND HAVING FUN

A s the 1970s dawned, a sunny little visage popped up on the American horizon. The happy face *(inset),* with its mile-wide smile and hopeful eyes, wanted nothing more than for everybody to feel good. In contrast to the passions of the '60s, this bland little emblem seemed to capture the ethos of the new decade—the quest for an easier time, a time, as the term went, without "hassle."

The freedom to "do your own thing" espoused by the young of the previous decade spread to virtually every corner of popular culture in the '70s, producing in many Americans a heady appetite for experimentation. Marriages split and the birthrate dwindled as people took to publicly discussing modes of behavior that would have been unthinkable a few years earlier. Baseball players swapped wives; a film star chatting with Johnny Carson on *The Tonight Show* might mention her recent pot bust as casually as her latest movie. The Moral Majority was outraged and tried to tighten its grip on the status quo.

Amid all the confusing options the decade offered, Americans seemed agreed on one purpose: having fun. Weary perhaps of the life-and-death issues of the recent past, they turned their attention from the front page to the style section. They snapped up fads, reveled in celebritydom, and, in a very real sense, tried on a new cultural wardrobe.

Emerging from the Pacific Ocean dripping wet in the 1979 movie 10, actress Bo Derek (left) only had to look gorgeous to become a pop icon for the end of the decade.

People Making News

"Personality journalism" is how Dick Stolley, the founding editor of *People,* described its unique blend of intimate reporting and dramatic photography. Mia Farrow graced the magazine's first cover on March 4, 1974, dolled up as Daisy Buchanan in the much hyped film *The Great Gatsby.* Inside, *People* served up more than the gossip and secondhand speculation of fan magazines of the past. Glimpses of lives more glamorous, fascinating, and romantic than most Americans experienced were shaped by the personal story—the inspirational, the eccentric, the cautionary—behind the public image.

For fun, President Gerald Ford was photographed cooling off in a swimming pool, and a usually sober-faced Pope John Paul II was caught mugging for the camera. The magazine went beyond celebs; ordinary people told extraordinary stories that placed them, if only briefly, in the limelight. *People* proved irresistible to the reading public and rapidly became one of the most successful magazines of the '70s—or of any decade.

SCREEN

DAVID CARRADINE BAR
PAST THE CUCKOO'S N
BUT NOW SAYS HE IS GL

If the good folks of Malibu's overpriced Carbon Mesa colony felt uneasy when carousing rocker Roger McGuinn was in residence, imagine the there-goes-the-neighborhood panic after he split and McGuinn's ex, Linda, took up with actor David Carradine. David, after all, had logged 500 acid trips and become the scourge of his old Laurel Canyon lair. A couple of years ago he trashed a nearby home (starkers) and later, while still on probation, was fined $20,000 for assaulting a local woman. Carradine also sired by his common-law lady, Barbara Seagull, a son they named Free, because father felt that "people were repressed at the time."

Yet lest the solid burghers of Carbon Mesa get uptight, David takes a squint at Linda's $300,000 estate and reassures: "With my tendencies as an anarchist and a revolutionary, this is the kind of place I would have wanted to blow up with a bomb in a paper

bag. Bu
where I
Castro
ilations
to be ei
Carradi
have cle
cept for
dope, he
marry he
als and i
hunting

Also, p
career is
befitting
won the
Motion P
Bound fo
phy of po
Guthrie. (
ture Acad
star but p
this year.)

It bugs
though a
phy, has b

Daily practice, says ABC's 'Kung Fu' alum David Carradine, exercises "demons, fears, stupidity and anger."

Carradine
empathetic
not a rebel.

Ingmar Bergman gambled on David in 'The Serpent's Egg' "because he has the princely blood of his father in his veins."

Photographs by Julian Wasser

51

Outtasight! An L.A. orthodontist invents invisible braces
The brave nun who preached to the Pope
People weekly
CHER
She and KISS's GENE SIMMONS bare their life together and marriage thoughts for the first time

JOCKS

FOR A SONG

LOOKS LIKE BARRY MANILOW'S MADE IT, TO SAY THE LEAST, BUT WHY ISN'T HE HAPPIER?

He writes the songs the whole world sings, but Barry Manilow still feels sort of miserable. He's the king of jingles (Band-Aids, Chevrolet) and the producer-arranger maestro who helped establish Bette Midler. Since he went solo, he has had eight hit singles in two years, including Grammy nominees *Mandy* and *I Write the Songs* and his current *Looks Like We Made It*. All five of his LPs have gone at least gold. "But to himself, Barry's still zero," says a former boyfriend. "He can't believe how enormous a star he is, and he's afraid it's all going to fall apart."

"I'm from nowhere, Brooklyn, up from nothing. I've worked my ass off to get here," is Barry's response, "and I'm gonna work my ass off to stay here. I can't sleep at night for the music going round in my head." That, of course, has gotten in the way of relationships with either sex, including the marriage with his high-school honey that dissolved after a year at age 22.

Now in his mid-30s (he claims to be younger), Manilow's success has made him a virtual recluse, terrified that fans will discover his address or phone number (which is more guarded even than Streisand's). Surrounding himself with an impenetrable buffer of go-betweens (not to mention a bulky blond chauffeur-bodyguard), Manilow never ventures out to movies and rarely to restaurants. "Anybody who really needs to can get to me," he maintains. "I'm a very private person. I don't want to share my life with anybody."

But he does share his home, lately renting what he calls "a ridiculous Beverly Hills palazzo" while at work on a new album and a 1978 TV special on the Coast. Present housemates include his general manager, manager, longtime friend Linda Allen, and his beloved pet beagle, "Bagel." But when his current projects are finished in the fall, Barry will skedaddle back to New York and the new West Side co-op whose roster so far includes only Linda and ... everybody in the music ... lives out here in L.A.," he

Beagle Bagel's master's voice has no

Photographs by Steve Schapiro/Sygma

Rock's Little Richard: from sin to salvation
JANUARY 8, 1979 • 75¢
People weekly
How old is man? Ask Richard Leakey
Sybil's shrink diagnoses a rapist with 10 personalities
Body Snatchers prey, Brooke Adams
It's SUPERMAN!
And it's Chris Reeve in the cape because McQueen was too fat, Stallone too Italian, Redford too expensive and Eastwood too busy

IN THIS ISSUE
Alice Cooper
The Jekyll and Hyde of glitter rock
Golfer Johnny Miller
The money's great—now on to the Masters
Pat Nixon
Who was the mystery man at her side?
Planner Ian McHarg
Put a tub on your roof to heat the house
Chris Evert and Jimmy Connors
Rich, in love—and happily square
Actor-Playwright Jason Miller
My ambition can frighten women
Minnie Pearl
Grand Ole Opry moves to fancy new digs
Lt. Col. Stirm's Divorce
A bitter end to a POW reunion
Lt. Hiroo Onoda
29 years in the jungle
Claude and Paloma Picasso
A French court makes them millionaires
Composer Marvin Hamlisch
Ann-Margret and Liza love him—does Oscar?
People weekly
April 1, 1974
35 Cents
Gerry Ford
The front-runner who promised not to run

IT'S FALL AND THE 1979 MODELS ARE COMING OUT, SO TAKE A LOOK AT THIS NEW FORD NAMED BETTY

..., almost everybody agreed, a tri... of the surgeon's skill. Oh, a ...ch here and there suggested that ... side was higher than the other, or ... her cheeks looked swollen. But ...a Barrett spoke for the multitudes ...ws in itself) when she enthused to ...lly Bergen, "She looks abso-lute-ly ...ee-you-tiful."

The cynosure at a $250-a-couple ...vening at Century City in L.A. was former First Lady Betty Ford, appearing in public for the first time since undergoing plastic surgery.

"I'm 60 and I want a nice new face to go with my beautiful new life," Mrs. Ford announced last month with the same marvelous candor that led her to talk openly about her breast cancer operation and her problems with drugs and alcohol.

The unveiling took place at an ANTA West benefit performance of *Annie*, followed by a champagne supper honoring Fred Astaire. Celebrities abounded; the star of the evening was Mrs. Ford. With her hair lightened to a honey blond, she wore an iridescent electric-blue chiffon gown. "I feel like a million dollars," she said, which may be close to the advance she reportedly landed for her memoirs, *The Times of My Life*, to be published next month.

And how does the former President like the new Betty Ford? "Jerry Ford's like most husbands," said one congressional pal fondly. "He's happy with anything that makes her happy that doesn't require too much of his time." □

Before and after: above, as Mrs. Ford appeared in May this year, and at right, with her new visage. One friend admired it, but confessed, "I couldn't stand the pain."

Annie Lockhart is third-generation Hollywood. Mom is June of *Lassie* fame, her granddad was character actor Gene.

Daffy Diversions

Fads sprouted in the '70s. President Carter's brew-swigging brother Billy got his own brand of beer. A holiday gift for 1975 was the Pet Rock, in its own carrying case. Mood rings promised to display their wearers' true feelings. Kids munched Pop Rocks, a candy that exploded in the mouth. CB radios *(opposite, bottom)* gained a following among truckers and other good buddies, spawning a new language of the road. Wackiest of all were streakers—people who dashed past outdoor crowds in the altogether.

A bobby politely employs his helmet to shield English rugby fans from the sight of a streaker's private parts. Nude sprints in public became a hilarious phenomenon shortly after a streaker interrupted actor David Niven's monologue at the globally televised 1974 Academy Awards show.

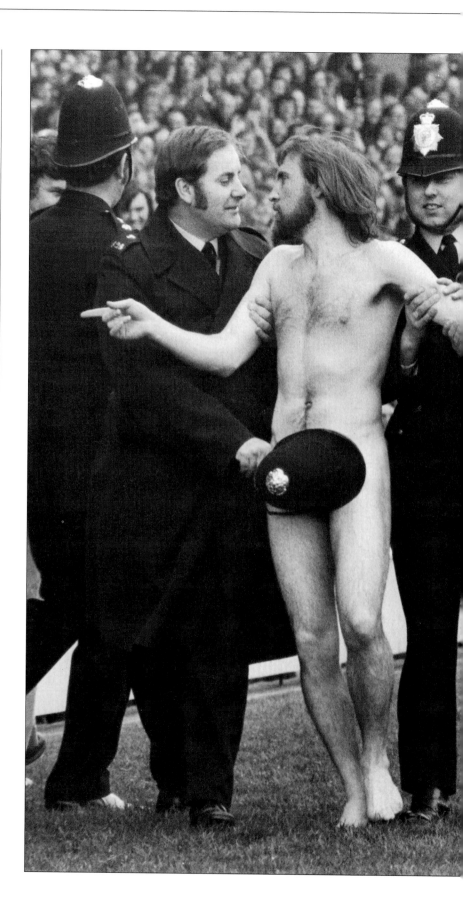

Seventies-Speak

In the '70s lexicon "dyne-o-mite" meant fabu-lous, "get down" meant get serious, and "laid back" was the opposite of "uptight." Newly coined words and phrases like those below hint-ed at what Americans were thinking and doing.

Biological clock (1978): internal timer ticking away a woman's childbearing years.

Birth mother (1975): the biological, not adoptive, parent.

Come out (1975): to declare one's homosexuality.

Palimony (1978): what you sue for when your live-in significant other *(see below)* dumps you.

Personal trainer (1975): a fitness coach who makes house calls.

Psychobabble (1977): language laden with words such as *self-actualize, denial,* and *enabler.*

Pump iron (1977): to lift weights.

Quality time (1977): uninterrupted inter-action with a spouse or child.

Rehab (1978): recovery from chemical dependence.

Significant other (1977): an individual with whom one is cohabitating or otherwise romantically involved.

Breaking Taboos

How Americans viewed sexual relations between consenting adults changed radically during the '70s as premarital, extramarital, interracial, and same-sex relations suddenly became more public and more accepted. As early as 1970 at Oberlin, Stanford, Michigan State, and a few other schools, male and female students started sharing dormitories. In 1972 Dr. Alex Comfort published his "gourmet guide to lovemaking," *The Joy of Sex (inset)*, and Americans made it a bestseller.

During the decade, the number of unmarried couples establishing households tripled to 1.6 million. Four-fifths of males and two-thirds of females had engaged in sexual relations by the age of 19. Not surprisingly, the number of teenage pregnancies jumped to one million a year by 1978.

America's tolerance for seemingly unconventional sexual arrangements moved past other barriers as well. The increased interaction of blacks and whites on the job, in the military, and in classrooms led to more interracial dating and marriage. Homosexuals grew more open about their lives, and Americans learned that among gay men and lesbians, nearly two-thirds had monogamous relationships. But the public wasn't ready to sanction same-sex marriage.

The interracial couple above met and began a romance in the sympathetic milieu of the University of Minnesota campus. Some mixed couples, moving to or starting out in a less liberal environment, learned that public acceptance of such relationships was still a work in progress.

When a New York City government clerk refused to issue marriage licenses to homosexuals in 1971, gay activists protested by delivering to his office a wedding cake decorated with figures of same-sex couples (right).

An unmarried couple at the University of Colorado frolic in a bathtub for a Life photographer in 1977, giving a distinctively '70s spin to the old idea of good clean fun.

The Peacock Revolution

Men's fashions in the '70s exploded in an outburst of color and flamboyance not seen since the heyday of the French monarchy. Men whose entire business wardrobe just a few years before ran the gamut from navy to gray now paraded to work in bold, bright plaids. And some suits, though they might not be worn to the office, sported patterned linings and nipped-in waists and were made of opulent fabrics like velvet and silk. Neckties widened and brightened with floral patterns, flopping down the pastel shirt fronts of all but the most uptight businessmen.

On vacation or on weekends, men abandoned neckties altogether and unbuttoned their shirts. Long shirt collars flared out over even wider lapels. A man with enough cash and confidence might wear a fur coat, and many fashion-conscious men donned leather coats or tight leather pants.

The '70s man could accessorize to his heart's content, having his pick of chunky belts, gold chains, and shoulder bags. Many staggered around in platform shoes. A store in Milwaukee offering high-heeled men's shoes sold an astounding 1,300 pairs in three months in 1971. Predictably, walking in them required adjustments. As one wearer observed—and as any woman could have told him—"They do tilt you a little."

Men's platform shoes

Outfits like this flap-pocketed, yellow polyester leisure suit and multicolored spread-collar shirt (above) made a statement about '70s casual attire for some men.

"I feel like a damn fool."

A '70s fight fan arrives at Madison Square Garden in full plumage. His brown fur suit emerges from under a cape lined in breathtaking geometrics.

Fashion Goes Democratic

The newly independent and assertive '70s woman, who made up her own mind about her career and her domestic life, carried this attitude over into her choice of clothes as well. She no longer meekly followed the dictates of the fashion industry.

When couturiers tried to put across a midcalf length called the midi in 1970, American women shunned the style, because it was unflattering on almost everyone. On the other hand, a welcome event for the growing number of women working outside the home was the mid-decade appearance of designer Diane von Furstenberg's versatile wrap and jersey dresses. These "bourgeois dresses" flattered most figures and looked smart both at the office and on a dinner date. Long pants for any occasion arrived in the form of the pants suit, a look borrowed from men's wear and touted as an expression of gender equality.

Near decade's end, women began raiding men's closets for baggy chinos, Oxford shirts, and wide neckties in response to the catch-as-catch-can style of Diane Keaton in the film *Annie Hall*. At the same time, blue jeans became high fashion as designers stitched their brand names onto a back pocket, inaugurating the era of designer clothes. Cowboy boots completed the look.

Frye boots

Life cover on '70s hemlines *(left)*

The *Annie Hall* look *(above)*

The advent of designer jeans *(above)*

Diane von Furstenberg *(above)*

Tube top and slave bracelet *(left)*

Decked out in red plastic five-inch platform sandals and white hot pants, this long-legged blonde beauty possessed the ideal figure to wear cutting-edge '70s fashions.

Fashion models (above) formed the glamorous core of New York's '70s disco scene. Tall, slender, and impossibly beautiful, they dressed—or undressed—in outfits that exhibited their carefully tended bodies to best advantage, treating the mirrored environs of the exclusive clubs like runways.

Gilded and costumed for a night at the Manhattan disco Xenon, a couple writhing in uninhibited self-absorption (right) appear to have entered their own euphoric fantasyland. Preparations for going out to a disco could reach outlandish extremes.

Disco

A new dance craze overtook America in the '70s, making nightlife one big—and sometimes decadent—party. Combining black rhythm and blues music and the Latino sound popular with Hispanics and gays, the thumping beat of disco was embraced by a generation hell-bent on ecstasy. At first confined to a few hedonistic after-hours clubs, disco quickly went mainstream.

Ground zero for disco was Studio 54, a former theater and CBS sound stage on Manhattan's West Side. Outside the entrance every Saturday night, a mob of hopefuls pressed against velvet ropes, beseeching the bouncers who guarded the doors to let them in. Inside, drugs were ubiquitous, clothing was optional. Several times a night, a cartoonlike "Man in the Moon" descended from the rafters, an enormous coke spoon full of twinkling lights floating to his nose in mimicry of the activity of choice occurring in the restrooms and on the balcony.

The dance floor was the former stage. On it, occasionally, could be glimpsed one of the privileged in-crowd—Bianca Jagger, Diana Ross, Liza Minnelli, Truman Capote, Andy Warhol—who often disappeared through a discreet door to the VIP room in the basement. Nor was it unusual to see a distinguished face like that of Israeli military hero Moshe Dayan, or even a dark-suited Republican senator. President Carter's mother, Miss Lillian, remarked after her visit, "I don't know if I was in heaven or hell. But it was *wonderful.*"

John Travolta as aspiring dancer Tony Manero pirouettes on the strobe-lighted floor of a blue-collar Brooklyn disco in the 1977 film Saturday Night Fever. By the end of the decade, disco palaces had popped up in neighborhoods across America.

Women on the Move

★

THE FEMINIST REVOLUTION

The civil rights movement showed how oppressed minorities could demand full participation in American democracy. Now, in the 1970s, the largest oppressed minority in America—so large it was actually a majority—was mobilizing. "Nobody can argue any longer about the rights of women," said activist and playwright Lillian Hellman. "It's like arguing about earthquakes."

The movement could trace its intellectual underpinnings to Betty Friedan's groundbreaking 1963 book, *The Feminine Mystique.* Writing of what she called "the problem that has no name," Friedan described the suburban lives of many American housewives as "comfortable concentration camps," where they lived out roles based solely on their sex and were denied chances to develop their talents.

Three years later Friedan helped found the National Organization for Women (NOW). The group's agenda included equal pay for equal work, access to more-desirable and better-paying "men's" jobs, legal abortion, and publicly funded childcare. "Women's liberation," as the media soon labeled the new movement, was about to forever change American viewpoints—including male disparagement of women going all the way back to biblical Eden *(inset).*

Linked in feminist solidarity, the vanguard of a 50,000-strong force of women marches down New York's Fifth Avenue on August 26, 1970, at the first annual nationwide Women's Strike for Equality.

The '70s began with women fighting for the Equal Rights Amendment (ERA). First introduced in Congress in 1923, the ERA would make it illegal to treat men and women differently solely because of sex. After many false starts the amendment was finally passed in 1972 and sent to the states for ratification.

In 1977 the ERA was only three votes shy of becoming part of the Constitution, but progress ground to a halt. The amendment had run into a storm of opposition, primarily from STOP ERA, an organization headed by a conservative Republican mother of six from Illinois, Phyllis Schlafly, who claimed that the ERA would bring about tax-funded abortion, homosexual marriage, the drafting of girls into the army, and unisex toilets.

In February 1978, with the ratification deadline

Displaying the text of the ERA, demonstrators rally at the U.S. Capitol on July 9, 1978, for extension of the ratification deadline.

"This is not a bedroom war, this is a political movement."

Betty Friedan

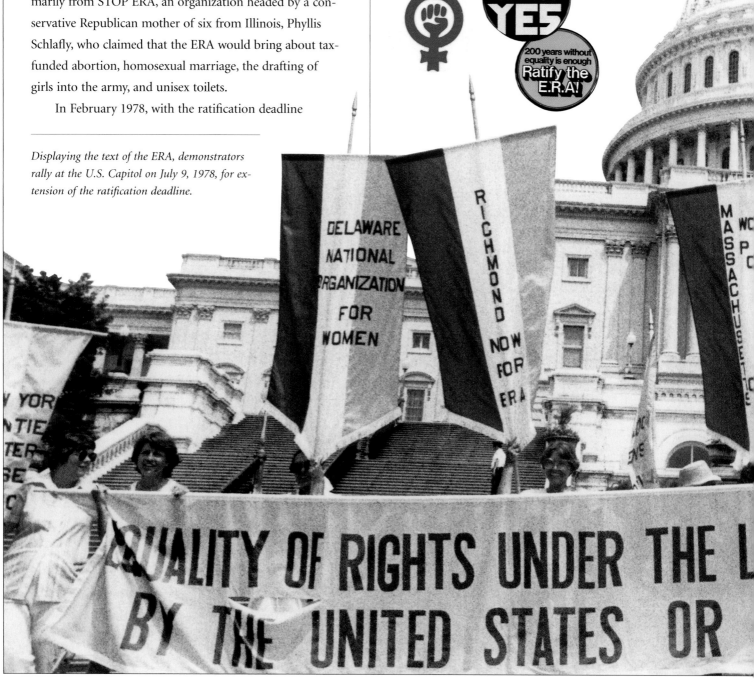

Phyllis Schlafly, chairperson of STOP ERA, galvanized nationwide conservative sentiment behind the belief that the ERA and other feminist legislation would destroy the integrity of the American family.

near, NOW organized women to campaign for an extension. The big push worked, and on October 6 Congress extended the deadline to 1982. But Schlafly's anti-ERA effort was also bearing fruit; enthusiasm for the amendment in state legislatures—even some that had already ratified it—was waning. Eventually, time would run out on the ERA.

Other legislative initiatives in the feminist program did better. Women won the passage of Title IX of the Education Amendments (1972), which outlawed sex discrimination in federally assisted education; and the Equal Credit Opportunity Act (1974), which banned the withholding of credit on the basis of sex or marital status. But equality before the law did not always mean equality in practice; for women's liberation these were just the first steps down a long road.

The Body Politic

Norma McCorvey, 21, divorced, and the mother of a five-year-old, walked into Columbo's Pizza in Dallas and sat down with two young female attorneys. It was December 1969, and McCorvey was three or four months into an unwanted pregnancy. No one knew it at the time, but she was about to assume a new identity that would become part of the American popular vocabulary: She was soon to be Jane Roe, of *Roe v. Wade.*

On January 22, 1973, McCorvey won one of the most sweeping and controversial legal decisions of the century when the Supreme Court ruled that women must be allowed the choice of a safe and legal abortion. The ruling marked the end of an era when women were driven to terminating unwanted pregnancies through criminal and dangerous back-alley procedures. Many Americans, however, abhorred the decision. Religious groups held that life begins at conception. Conservatives feared that legalizing abortion would promote promiscuity and undermine families. But for feminists, *Roe v. Wade* represented one of the major milestones in women's age-old struggle to win control over what happened to their bodies. Highlighting the feminist viewpoint, author and activist Lucinda Cisler wrote, "The real question is not, 'How can we justify abortion?' but, 'How can we justify compulsory childbearing?'"

Abortion rights was just one battleground in this war; another was the issue of violence. The movement drew

Lying in a coffin surrounded by pro-choice slogans, a demonstrator in August 1973 plays the role of a woman who died from a home abortion. Although Roe v. Wade had been the law of the land for seven months by then, feminists continued to campaign against an antiabortion backlash.

attention to such previously "invisible" crimes as rape and battery. Women Against Violence Against Women and similar groups mounted media campaigns denouncing what they saw as society's willingness to condone and even encourage physical assaults on women. Feminists founded rape crisis centers and started self-defense classes throughout the country.

Thanks to the heightened consciousness engendered by the feminist movement, women also began reclaiming their physiological and sexual selves from a male-dominated medical establishment. Home births and gynecological self-exams became more prevalent. Pregnancy was reinterpreted not as an "illness," the domain of medicine, but as a natural process in which a woman could play a decision-making role.

Author Robin Morgan (right) trains in a Manhattan women's karate class. Self-defense was one of the ways women resisted rape.

> ## "If men could get pregnant, abortion would be a sacrament."
>
> Florynce Kennedy

First published in 1971, Our Bodies, Ourselves sold more than three million copies by 1979. It covered such topics as pregnancy, rape, birth control, and menopause from a woman's perspective.

Outraged over police complacency toward rape in New York City, women demonstrate to spotlight the true nature of the crime.

A Revolution in Print

Early on the morning of March 18, 1970, a group of about 75 women gathered purposefully at Saint Peter's Lutheran Church in New York City. At their head was feminist writer Susan Brownmiller. The group's destination—the offices of the glossy, high-circulation *Ladies' Home Journal.*

Carrying posters reading "Women's Liberated Journal," Brownmiller and her troops arrived at the magazine's headquarters and crowded into the office of editor John Mack Carter, determined to remain until their demands were met. Protesting the demeaning image of women portrayed in fashion magazines and the lowly roles of women staff members on the magazines, they demanded the naming of a woman editor in chief for the *Journal,* a day-care center for employees' children, a ban on denigrating or exploitative ads, and the publication of an issue edited entirely by feminists. Insults flew. Someone threatened to overturn filing cabinets. And by midmorning 200 more women had arrived. The "siege," as Carter referred to it, lasted 11 hours. In the end, Carter agreed to publish an eight-page feminist supplement to be inserted in the August issue. The *Journal* didn't really change, but the sit-in, the press coverage it received, and the resulting supplement were a start.

Media coverage of the women's movement became increasingly balanced as the decade progressed, moving from the patronizing 1970 Time cover headlined "Kate Millett of Women's Lib" to the 1976 issue picturing 12 women as the 1975 Women of the Year.

"A woman without a man is like a fish without a bicycle."

Gloria Steinem

Gloria Steinem, founding editor of Ms., addresses the National Press Club in Washington, D.C., in December 1977. The display behind her satirizes President Jimmy Carter.

Representing a new generation of feminists, seven-year-old Tara MacNeil samples the wares at New Words Bookstore, a shop run by women in Cambridge, Massachusetts.

Another feminist writer, Gloria Steinem, was looking for an independent way to give voice to women's issues. Almost two years after Brownmiller staged her sit-in, Steinem helped found a magazine dedicated to the women's movement. It took its name from the title women were increasingly using to avoid being identified by their marital status—"Ms." The first issue hit the newsstands in December 1971 and sold 250,000 copies in eight days. *Ms.* would go on to become a staple of its day, running articles and advertisements that reflected and promoted the dramatic changes occurring in women's lives.

GOD IS COMING AND IS SHE PISSED

Mainstream magazines such as *Time*, *Life*, *Newsweek*, and the *Atlantic Monthly* also began writing about the women's movement, although not all the early coverage pleased feminists. When Kate Millett, author of 1970's *Sexual Politics,* made the cover of *Time (opposite, top)* as a symbol of the entire movement, she was disgusted, having argued that the cover should represent diverse faces involved in feminist politics.

The 1970s also saw a boom in books written by and about women. In addition to Millett's groundbreaking treatise were Robin Morgan's *Sisterhood Is Powerful*, Germaine Greer's *The Female Eunuch,* Erica Jong's *Fear of Flying,* Susan Brownmiller's *Against Our Will,* and Marilyn French's *The Women's Room*. A new kind of enterprise, the women's bookstore, not only sold these publications to a female clientele but also served as a meeting place for the growing sisterhood of local activists.

Women at Work

For every dollar a man made in the '70s, a woman made 59 cents. A woman with a college degree earned less, on average, than a man with an eighth-grade education. Nevertheless, women were increasingly taking jobs outside the home. More than half of all American families in 1978 had two or more wage earners.

But women got almost no crack at high-skill and managerial positions. About four-fifths were segregated in low-paying clerical, sales, service, or factory jobs. Of the 1,300 largest companies in the United States, only two were headed by women. "If you aren't born white and male in America," wrote Gloria Steinem, "you are statistically likely to end up as some sort of support system for those who are."

To break this pattern, women had to confront resistance both subtle and blatant. Women aspiring to space exploration, for example, faced attitudes like that of astronaut James Lovell, who said, "We fully envision . . . that in the near future, we will fly women into space and use them the same way we use them on Earth—and for the same purpose." Fighting such attitudes, women pushed their way into jobs as doctors, chefs, construction workers, and auto mechanics.

Feminists were also reexamining the very nature of work. No longer, they argued, was work only what men did outside the home; now it meant all kinds of labor, including housework.

Demonstrators at International Women's Day in New York City in 1977 campaign for pay for the work women do in the home. Society's failure to value the labor that women contributed to their households carried over into the marketplace, holding down pay scales for domestic employees doing cleaning, cooking, and laundry. At right, three miners in Vansant, Virginia, in 1976 pose after a day's labor at a new kind of women's work.

A Boston Marathon official tries to eject a woman from the 1967 race but is blocked by a male runner. Women were barred from the marathon—they were considered too frail—but Katherine Switzer got in by using her initial rather than her first name when registering by mail. Two miles into the race, officials discovered that "K. Switzer" was a woman. Although she finished unharmed, it took another five years before the Boston Marathon was officially opened to women.

Tasting the Joy of Big-Time Sports

When Billie Jean King won her first Wimbledon singles title in 1966, the prize was a gift certificate for clothes. Women's professional tennis, like most opportunities for women in sports, was severely limited and poorly rewarded. But King's aggressive play and powerful personality revolutionized her sport so profoundly that in 1971 she won $100,000—more than any other American tennis player that year, male or female.

Then, in 1973, King was involved in an event that would change the way people looked at all women's sports.

Lunging for a ball, Billie Jean King displays the same fierce drive she employed in battling for the advancement of women in sports.

Bobby Riggs, a 55-year-old former tennis champion with a wisecracking sexist attitude, challenged King to a match. "The battle of the sexes" drew a TV audience estimated at 50 million. King handily defeated her over-the-hill opponent in three straight sets. The match had an enormous impact, promoting new respect for female athletes.

About the same time, women's athletics acquired a powerful legislative weapon in the form of a seemingly innocuous item called Title IX. Enacted in 1972, it was designed to give women equal access to educational programs. It quickly came to be used, however, to require universities to fund women's sports on a par with men's. Despite angry resistance at many of the sports-powerhouse schools, the new law promoted tremendous growth in women's college athletics.

> "Let the best man win, whomever she may be."
>
> Helen Meyner

Young girls try out for Little League in Hoboken, New Jersey, in 1974. New Jersey was the first state to open Little League to girls.

Lady Bird Johnson, Rosalynn Carter, Betty Ford, and conference chair Bella Abzug (left to right) pass the torch to a younger generation at the First National Women's Conference in Houston in 1977.

"We Will Not Be Divided"

L et us make it clear that we will not be divided in our struggle to gain the simple fairness our country stands for around the world," said Judy Carter, President Carter's daughter-in-law, in her remarks at the First National Women's Conference. The conference brought together a politically diverse group of 20,000 women.

"I was never more proud to be a woman."

Bella Abzug, 1977

"It was like a supermarket checkout line from Anywhere, U.S.A., . . ." wrote *Ms.* magazine reporter Lindsy Van Gelder, "homemakers and nuns, . . . secretaries and farmers and lawyers, mahogany skins and white and café au lait. We were an all-woman Carl Sandburg poem come to life."

The conferees drew up a national plan of action, forwarding to the president and to Congress a legislative program calling for the passage of ERA; Medicaid-funded abortion, childbirth, and prenatal care; and laws barring antigay discrimination. Ten years earlier, such goals would have been considered extremist; by 1977 they were mainstream.

International Women's Equality Symbol

Mainstream Music Runs Wild

★

THE SPLINTERED SOUND OF THE 70S

When Jimi Hendrix burned his guitar to end his performance at the 1967 Monterey International Pop Concert, he was unwittingly signaling the approaching end of a musical era. "After you set your guitar on fire," said guitarist Danny Kootch, "what do you have left? Set fire to yourself? It had to go the other way." Kootch had the right idea, but music actually went in many directions during the '70s. In the 1960s, as Columbia Records president Clive Barnes observed in 1973, "one kind of music absorbed everything else. Now the universe of music is expanding on all fronts."

The rock and pop scene fragmented into a kaleidoscope of new genres—hard rock, soft rock, heavy metal, punk, funk, reggae, rap—each with its own sound and its own style. There was something for everyone, from the lushly sentimental Carpenters *(inset)* to the theatrical shock-rock band Kiss *(left)*—and even beyond *(pages 128-129)*. Music was liberated from its '60s role as a vehicle for changing the world. Instead, an old sentiment reemerged: Music is entertainment, and rock performers the entertainers.

Was the new music all fluff, as many critics claimed? Or was it just a reflection of those uncertain times? Whether or not people liked the sounds of the '70s, the music left a legacy of fine song writing, magical technology, outrageous spectacle, and even a sense of humor.

Faces made up for shock effect, the members of Kiss perch like animated gargoyles atop the Empire State Building. The band used bizarre antics onstage, such as breathing fire and spewing fake blood.

Songs of Myself: The New Troubadours

The early '70s saw the emergence of a crop of introspective singer-songwriters. Many of them, like Toronto-born Neil Young *(right),* were émigrés from the 1960s folk-music scene. Young's confessional ballads resonated with a huge body of fans, one of whom was singer Joni Mitchell, who became the quintessential practitioner of the art and even composed a song for Young. "The most important thing is to write in your own blood," Mitchell said in 1974. "I bare intimate feelings because people should know how other people feel."

Young and Mitchell had lots of company. Between 1970 and 1973 scores of young troubadours launched "concept albums," candid self-portraits in the form of a dozen or so songs. Though they were all skilled song crafters, their approaches varied: James Taylor and Carly Simon, like Joni Mitchell, wrote intensely personal lyrics. Randy Newman, Loudon Wainwright III, and John Prine turned to humor. Romantic visionaries Laura Nyro and Tom Waits rewrote personal experience as mythology. And that master of versatility, Paul Simon, after splitting with Art Garfunkel, did it all.

In Los Angeles, sophisticated recording studios transformed the intimacy of the singer-songwriter's work into California pop rock. Jackson Browne, Linda Ronstadt, the Eagles, and Fleetwood Mac all produced definitive versions of this softer rock that pushed aside the harder-edged music of the '60s. The pop rockers made southern California's Laurel Canyon their playground. They hung out together, sat in on one another's recording sessions, and sometimes had romantic liaisons—which inspired still more songs.

But by the late '70s, L.A. had lost its mellow feel, and troubadours were on the way out. They were partly undermined by the rise of punk rock and disco, but they also simply ran out of things to say about themselves.

Sequestered in a cabin on his Broken Arrow Ranch in northern California, a contemplative 26-year-old Neil Young takes a break from writing songs for his 1972 album Harvest.

Little Big Man of Rock

"I didn't start enjoying life until I was 21, so I'm living through my teenage period now."

Elton John, 1978

Camp to his toes, Elton John wore these show-stopping silver leather boots, monogrammed with huge Es and Js, in 1973. The five-foot, eight-inch performer preferred platform soles and stacked heels for the three inches or so that they added to his height.

Surely no one could have predicted that Reginald Dwight—a short, pudgy, balding, and bespectacled Brit—would become the piano-pumping rock giant known as Elton John. His romantic sensibility and unerring musical instincts, combined with campy costumes and an act that was wild but not too decadent, created an infectious style of pop music that sold out stadiums and ruled the FM dial.

Dwight began playing the piano when he was four years old and won a scholarship to the Royal Academy of Music at age 11. During a teenage stint with the London backup band Bluesology, he chose a new name for himself in tribute to saxophonist Elton Dean and singer John Baldry.

In 1970 John made his now-legendary American debut in L.A. at the Troubadour, performing handstands on the keyboard, among other antics, while singing up a storm. "People just went crazy," he reported. "The *Los Angeles Times* gave me the rave review of all time, and it spread across America and I became an overnight sensation."

With lyricist Bernie Taupin, John became a hit factory that lasted most of the decade. Taupin cranked out the words; John the chords and melody, always with exactly the right musical hook. The most successful singer-songwriter team since the Beatles' Lennon and McCartney, John and Taupin had six number one hits. Of their 19 albums, 15 went gold or platinum.

Rock superstar Elton John belts out his best to a sold-out crowd at Los Angeles's Dodger Stadium in 1975. John was the first act to play this immense venue since the Beatles in 1966.

One Nation Under a Groove

U sing clever lyrics, punchy instrumental arrangements, and
a booming bass line, recording
entrepreneur Berry Gordy's Motown label
entered the '70s as it had closed out the
previous decade—the trendsetter in black
pop music. Calling its music "the Sound
of Young America," the black-owned hit
factory was the most successful independent recording studio in the country.

The Motown sound appealed to both
blacks and whites, making the recordings
highly lucrative in both the rhythm and
blues and pop markets. For the '70s the
label's newest big act—which would also
be its last—was the Jackson 5. With six top-
five singles by 1971, including "ABC" and
"I Want You Back," the group of brothers
was fronted by wunderkind Michael Jackson *(right),* who turned 12 in 1970 and became the quintessential crossover superstar.

While the Jackson 5 were churning out
hits, older Motown stars began asking for
more artistic freedom to speak out on social issues such as prejudice and injustice.
Though a stalwart of Berry Gordy's tightly
controlled system, Marvin Gaye *(page 118)*
was one of the first to do so. "I dug the hip-
pies," said Gaye. "They had the imagination
to dress differently, think differently, rein-
vent the world for themselves. I loved that."

Gaye's rebellion against Gordy's party-
music-only policy took the form of a 1971
landmark album, *What's Going On?* To a

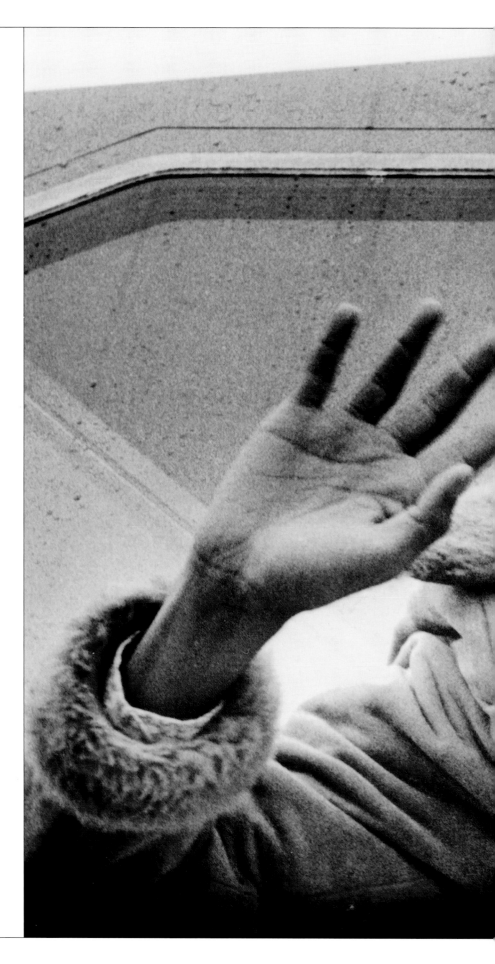

Ever eager to charm a crowd, 14-year-old Michael Jackson waves to London fans on a 1972 European tour for the release of his hugely successful first solo album, Got to Be There. A cut on the album about Ben, a pet rat, became a number one hit.

hushed sound and a conga beat, Gaye's plea for world harmony touched on the Vietnam War, inner-city problems, and the racial divide. As the album's sales soared, Gordy came to see that the times had changed. Indeed, about this time he went so far as to abandon Motown's Detroit roots and move the company to L.A.

Gaye's labelmate Stevie Wonder *(opposite)* also reinvented himself in the '70s. The blind child prodigy began to preach a message of unity. He masterfully interwove spiritual odes with songs of the street on his 1973 album *Innervisions,* performing cuts such as "Higher Ground" and "Living for the City" in a blues-style husky growl. Wonder's sound, borrowed from rhythm and blues, jazz, rock, and reggae, not only lit up Motown's recording studios but also contributed to virtuoso live performances. He was what the industry called a monster—an act guaranteed to pack the house.

Motown had no monopoly on change in '70s black music. Sexy soul singer Al Green *(right)* had his own approach, mixing gospel music with urban rhythm and blues to express universal themes of love and desire. His simple sound—strong backbeats riding quiet horns and strings over which floated Green's silky, sensual voice—helped shape the spirit of '70s soul.

Even the legendary James Brown, the self-proclaimed godfather of soul, was finding a new sound. "Heat the beat," said Brown, "and the rest'll turn sweet." He was talking about rhythm, not melody, which he derisively likened to "soapsuds and jingles."

Sly Stone *(inset, page 121)* took Brown's gutsy bass line and amplified it to

A honey-throated tenor with a three-octave range, Motown singer-songwriter Marvin Gaye (left) hit a new stride with the 1971 release of his album What's Goin' On?, a deeply personal take on social issues. His 1973 megahit "Let's Get It On" cemented his position as one of the sexiest voices of the decade.

Al Green (above) used gospel sounds, including gentle moans and a rising falsetto, in his romantic 1973 album Livin' for You. Ordained a minister in 1976, Green continued his pop-gospel career, selling more than 20 million records by decade's end.

Stevie Wonder works a packed house at Madison Square Garden in 1974, the year he won five Grammy awards. Blind since infancy and recording since the age of 12, Wonder broadened his already large following when he toured with the Rolling Stones in 1972.

George Clinton (left), sporting a wavy hairpiece, gets down with outlandishly garbed members of his combined Parliament/Funkadelic band in a 1977 concert. The funk group's tribal rhythms, elaborate stage props, and flamboyant finery contributed, said Clinton, to "saving dance music from the blahs."

the foreground. His racially mixed band, the Family Stone, invented a pop-soul-rock hybrid that had everyone dancing. A turning point for Stone came in 1971 with the release of the album *There's a Riot Goin' On*. Tense and militant, it featured syncopated rhythms that halted and faltered, sounding like "Muzak with its finger on the trigger," in the words of one music critic. The Family Stone's fusion of black rhythms with a psychedelic collage of chants, hooks, and shifting voices and instrumentation soon ushered in another innovation: funk.

Funk was pure black. It was the sound of the inner city getting down, driven by hard-rock guitar. Funk act Kool and the Gang mingled wild horns, jagged bass patterns, and party whoops, peaking in 1974 with the dance hits "Jungle Boogie" and "Hollywood Swinging." At the more restrained end of the funk spectrum, Earth, Wind and Fire mixed jazz, soul, and African folk elements to create the 1975 hit album *That's the Way of the World*.

Funk's most radical practitioner was George Clinton. To him, funk was "the way blacks act when they are together," and togetherness reigned in two bands he fronted—Parliament and Funkadelic *(left)*—which often performed as one. Clinton onstage was elaborate theater heavily dosed with science fiction. "That old theory of 'I'm cute, I'm a fad, I have a hit record and here it is' just doesn't go anymore in staging an act," he said. "Kids are too sophisticated today. They've paid their money, and they have a right to say, 'Now move me.' "

Clinton moved them with albums such as *Maggot Brain* and *Free Your Mind and Your Ass Will Follow*, as well as a flashy world tour. The act included stage antics featuring a hovering spaceship from which Clinton sometimes emerged nearly naked. So strong was the appeal of this fundamentally black music that all-white groups like Wild Cherry, Average White Band, and KC and the Sunshine Band were soon climbing on the funk bandwagon.

Disco the Night Away

Disco diva Donna Summer (above), dressed for the mood, cuts a dance recording. Her producers plotted her musical career note by note.

The Gibb brothers, aka the Bee Gees (above), singing falsetto harmonies, hit it big with their 1977 Saturday Night Fever soundtrack album.

Disco was the '70s music phenomenon everyone either loved or hated. Percolating up from New York's gay, black, and Latino subcultures, by mid-decade it pulsated into the pop mainstream, thanks partly to its disdain for the hard-rock guitar solos and power chords that were making nightclub music undanceable for many revelers.

Disco tunes were created in the recording studio specifically to get people out onto the floor. Produced to a relentless metronomic beat with a synthesizer, the songs featured overdubbing, percussive interludes, and violin—not guitar—riffs. Lightweight lyrics, sung mainly by female vocalists, encouraged listeners to boogie, get down, keep on dancing, and live it up.

Since the music came from a turntable, the disc jockey ruled the dance floor, orchestrating the music and lights to manipulate the mood. Record companies responded by producing album-size "disco singles" that ran far longer than the versions made for radio play and labeled them with "bpm"—beats per minute—so that DJs could mix selections smoothly.

With little occasion for live performances, few singers made a career out of disco. "Disco was a faceless music," said David Hodo, the "construction worker" of the Village People *(right)*. "We gave disco a face."

One of the few disco superstars, Donna Summer *(above, left)*, launched her career in 1975 by moaning and panting her way through a 17-minute soft-porn paean called "Love to Love You Baby," following it with the similarly suggestive "Bad Girls" and "Hot Stuff."

Only a handful of groups and solo artists enjoyed relatively lengthy careers. Chic made a splash with "Dance, Dance, Dance" and "Le Freak"; Barry White sang "Can't Get Enough of Your Love, Baby" and "You're the First, the Last, My Everything"; and the Bee Gees *(left)* proved to be the biggest act of all. Most disco blockbusters, however, were the products of one-hit wonders like Thelma Houston with "Don't Leave Me This Way" and Vicki Sue Robinson with "Turn the Beat Around."

At peak popularity in 1979, the Village People (right) cavorted on an April cover of Rolling Stone. The group emerged from the gay underground club scene and introduced their music and sensibility to the mainstream while parodying male stereotypes. Their goofy but danceable hits "Macho Man" and "Y.M.C.A" became disco favorites.

M14170 • APRIL 19TH, 1979

ISSUE NO. 289 • $1.00 UK 60P

Rolling Stone

FROM THE YMCA TO THE NAVY · BY ABE PECK
VILLAGE PEOPLE

GEORGE HARRISON: A CANDID CONVERSATION WITH THE QUIETEST BEATLE · BY MICK BROWN

DISCO REPORT: CHIC, STUDIO 54, ROLLER DISCO AND MORE....

HAIR: TONIC FOR THE '70s · BY JULIA CAMERON

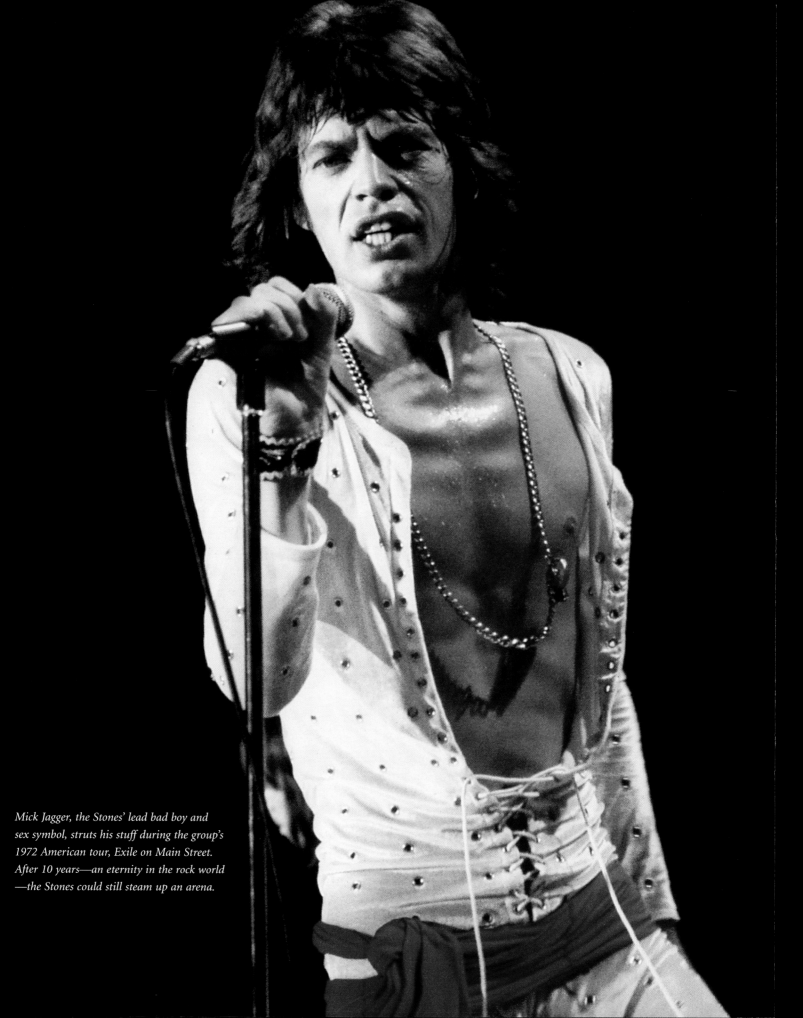

Mick Jagger, the Stones' lead bad boy and sex symbol, struts his stuff during the group's 1972 American tour, Exile on Main Street. After 10 years—an eternity in the rock world —the Stones could still steam up an arena.

It's Only Rock and Roll

I t was the summer of '72, and the Rolling Stones were back again, this time for their biggest concert tour yet. In eight weeks the Stones put on 50 concerts in 30 U.S. cities for 750,000 fans, some of whom had camped out for two days just to score tickets. Rock and roll—the Stones' version, at any rate—was alive and well.

With the Beatles disbanded, Dylan's impact ebbing, and Janis Joplin, Jimi Hendrix, and Jim Morrison gone from this world, the Stones were the last of the high-flying '60s rock gods. "I can't even *remember* the Beatles," said Mick Jagger *(opposite)* while on tour. "It seems so long ago. That was another era."

The Stones had not only escaped the fate of others, they had also become the industry's premier music machine. Their fans continued to demand the old blues-rooted rock that had made the band famous. "We have to accept," said Jagger, "what the people want." What they wanted

Singer Robert Plant (left) leads Led Zeppelin through a sizzling performance in L.A. in 1971. The bluesy solos and recording-studio innovations of guitarist Jimmy Page (right) helped set the group apart from imitators, who copied their thunderous volume, hammering beat, and near-chaotic arrangements.

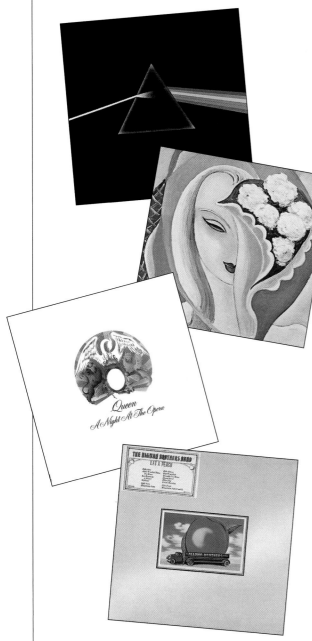

In the '70s albums, not singles, became the medium for serious rock. Classic releases included (from top) recordings by Pink Floyd, Eric Clapton's Derek and the Dominos, Queen, and the Allman Brothers.

In the guise of his alter ego, Ziggy Stardust, David Bowie (opposite) stages a climactic duet with sideman Mick Ronson's guitar. Commercial artist-turned-singer Bowie's often startling theatrics made him a creative giant of '70s rock.

wasn't only the music, but the Stones as a sociosexual event. "The point of [a Stones] concert," wrote essayist Robert Hughes in a 1972 issue of *Time,* "is the presence of Mick Jagger, who is still arguably the supreme sexual object in modern Western culture."

While the Stones remained prisoners of their past, Led Zeppelin *(page 125)* pioneered a new assault on the ears and viscera—the heavy-metal sound, which shaped hard rock for the rest of the decade. Formed during Britain's late-'60s blues-rock boom, Led Zeppelin took metal music—loud guitar, ear-shattering vocals, and macho posturing—and finessed its riffs with shades of the blues. Jimmy Page, the group's producer and virtuoso lead guitarist, was a genius with sound. He used distortion, feedback, echo, reverb, and sheer amplification to create rock as sculptured noise.

Led Zeppelin's lyrics set it apart, too. The group forayed into fantasy, myth, and the occult, bringing it all together in the unforgettable "Stairway to Heaven." Never released as a single, the song became the greatest hit in the history of album-oriented FM rock radio—and the decade's anthem.

Heavy metal wasn't the only hard rock getting FM airplay in the early '70s. Car radios blasted out the music of southern bands, like Georgia's Allman Brothers, who took rock back to the sounds and spirit of their native soil in *Eat a Peach,* and the classic rock of Eric Clapton's group, Derek and the Dominos, who hit it big with "Layla."

Progressive rock's most popular band, Pink Floyd, hit the album chart and stayed there for an unbelievable 741 weeks with its heavily synthesized breakthrough release, *The Dark Side of the Moon.* By mid-decade progressive rock was being taken to a new place by Queen's *A Night at the Opera*— a merger with a new form, glitter rock.

A slicker form of hard rock, glitter—or glam—was not so much a musical style as a fashion statement. Spawned in England in the early '70s, glitter glorified sexual ambiguity and androgyny. Self-consciously decadent, glam rockers wore foppish getups, lots of makeup, and glitter dust to tweak hard rock's macho poseurs. The aim was good theater, and no one put on a better show than David Bowie, the king of camp.

Through spectacle Bowie could make almost any fantasy compelling, including a self-made persona as a space alien-turned-rock star named Ziggy Stardust. In 1972 Bowie—orange-shagged, glam-fitted, androgynous, and shrill—brought his dazzling *Ziggy Stardust* show to America. It was a new twist: Rock as spectacle as sham. He opened the door for New York's glitter-rock underground, epitomized by the New York Dolls, a bridge group standing somewhere between glitter and punk rock *(pages 128-129).*

Anarchy Rules!

Raging against "corporate" rock from groups like the Rolling Stones, punk rock exploded from New York's arty East Village in the mid-'70s. Cruder than the music performed by the precursor groups Velvet Underground and the New York Dolls, punk featured manic rhythms, buzz-saw guitar work, and hoarse, screaming vocals. Punk rock started in clubs like CBGB that showcased new artists, among them Television and Patti Smith *(right)*, punk's own female revolutionary. Smith's rock clarion call to every garage band across the country: "We created it. Let's take it over."

Punk came in many styles. Blondie's pop sound had a flirty sexuality, while Talking Heads and Elvis Costello *(inset, left)* veered toward new-wave rock, punk's more sophisticated offshoot. Witty and spare, the Ramones *(inset, below)* shouted songs like "Now I Want to Sniff Some Glue." The Ramones became a catalyst for the appearance of British punk rock, a working-class uprising against the Establishment. "All we're trying to do is destroy everything," said Johnny Rotten of the Sex Pistols, the definitive British punk group.

But nothing so extreme could long endure, and punk began to decline in 1977. Johnny Rotten declared the movement dead the next year. His Sex Pistols partner, Sid Vicious *(opposite),* took the ethos of punk to its perhaps logical extreme, stabbing his girlfriend to death in 1978 and committing suicide a year later. The decade-long fragmenting of popular music was complete.

Kinetic punk-rock artist Patti Smith, a painter-turned-poet and sometime playwright, plays air guitar after her 1975 debut with the groundbreaking album Horses. Although she was implacably opposed to big-business rock, her singing was influenced by two of its biggest stars, Mick Jagger and the late Jim Morrison.

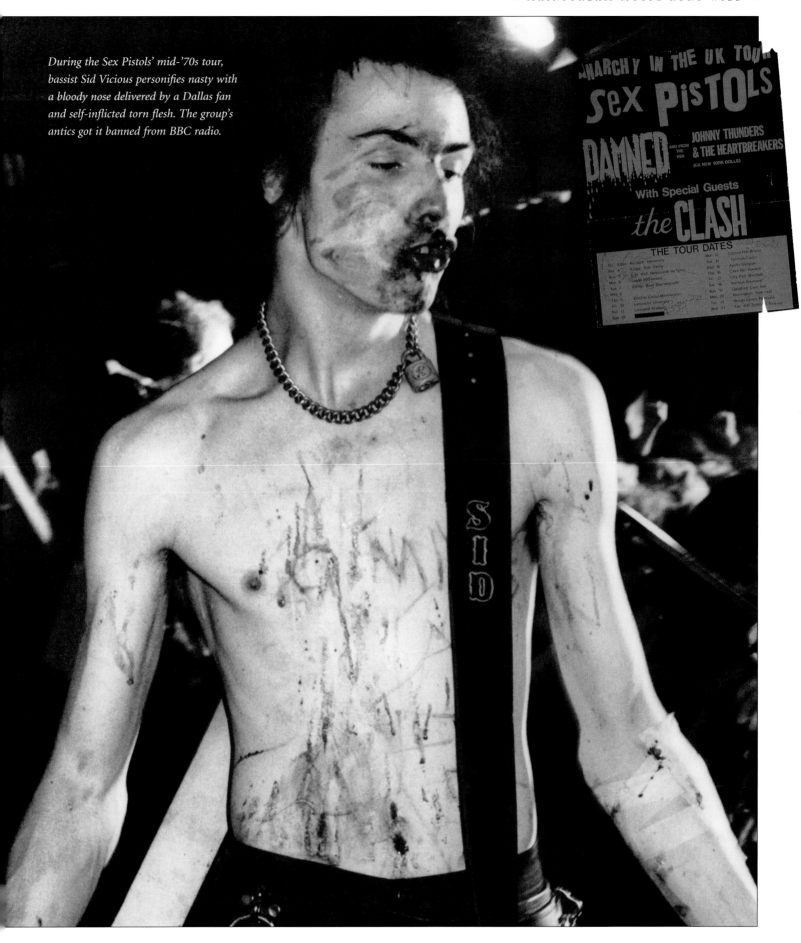

During the Sex Pistols' mid-'70s tour, bassist Sid Vicious personifies nasty with a bloody nose delivered by a Dallas fan and self-inflicted torn flesh. The group's antics got it banned from BBC radio.

Dark Side of the Decade

★

A LITANY OF WOE

"Have a nice day," Americans from coast to coast began saying to each other in the '70s. The expression soon became an empty mantra, and by decade's end it had taken on an unconscious irony: This period of our history, though it saw fewer of the kinds of white-hot issues that racked the previous decade, was nonetheless marked from the start by a number of distinctly un-nice days that occupied the headlines and tormented the soul.

The XX Olympiad at Munich in 1972 was meant to be "the Games of Joy," a celebration not only of Olympic sport but also of a prosperous, democratic Germany risen from the ashes of Nazism and war. They were every bit of that for 10 marvelous days, from August 25 until the dawning of September 5—destined to be one of the decade's unforgettably awful days. Eight Palestinian terrorists burst into the quarters of the Israeli Olympic team, killing two team members on the spot and taking nine others hostage.

The terrorists demanded the release of some 200 of their comrades from Israeli jails. The Israelis flatly refused, though they permitted German officials to go through the motions of negotiating. The standoff continued for 17 hours and ended in a tragic firefight at a German air force base, where a police ambush went horribly awry. The terrorists were all killed or captured, but not before they had murdered their nine hostages. How grotesque, lamented one sorrowing German, "to plan for light and earn darkness."

A hooded terrorist peers from the balcony of the Israeli rooms at the Munich Olympic Village in 1972. Security was so lax that the gunmen had only to go over one fence to breach the compound's defenses.

Firestorm of Rage at a Prison Hellhole

New York's Attica State Correctional Facility was a grim place. Behind its walls 2,250 convicts, crowded into a space meant for 1,600, festered in a racially poisoned environment. More than half the prisoners were black and 9 percent were Puerto Rican; 379 of the 380 guards were white. In July 1971 the inmates of this powder keg had asked state corrections commissioner Russell Oswald for 27 improvements, most of them modest: access to additional outside medical care—including Spanish-speaking doctors—at the inmates' expense, more than one shower a week, a baseball field, better food. Oswald found the demands reasonable but asked for time. Money was tight, he said.

On September 8 time ran out. A rumor swept through the prison that an inmate had struck a guard and gone unpunished. At first electrified by this apparent evidence of official weakness, the convicts then heard that the inmate had been thrown into solitary after a violent struggle in which he had been beaten. The next morning about 1,000 inmates erupted in riot, taking 40 prison personnel hostage and beating some of them severely.

The rioters soon released the most badly injured hostages and issued additional demands, stressing amnesty for the rioters. Authorities agreed to most of these, but one of the injured guards had died, and they would grant no amnesty. Accept what was offered, they said, or face having Attica retaken by force. The inmates stood their ground.

On September 13 Governor Nelson Rockefeller ordered 600 National Guardsmen to join Attica guards, local police, and state troopers in storming the prison. The assault left 39 men dead, including 10 hostages. Early reports said rioters had slit the hostages' throats, but it was soon shown that all the dead, including the hostages, had been shot by the attacking force.

The tragedy prompted a nationwide spate of attempts at reform. Given fiscal constraints and burgeoning prison populations, however, most of those efforts went nowhere. Attica itself became a byword, even among hardened convicts, for a particularly bad place to be.

Attica inmates raise clenched fists in support of the uprising. Along with the 29 convicts killed in the bloodbath that ended the rebellion, more than 80 were seriously injured. Three others had been killed by fellow inmates before the prison was stormed.

Skyjacking: A New Criminal Fad

The crime was so conveniently all-purpose—for profit, for political impact, for just about anything the perpetrator might have in mind. A person merely had to board an airliner, sit back until takeoff, then wave a gun at a flight attendant and announce an agenda. In a flash he would have command of the aircraft and control over the lives of terrified passengers and crew. This kind of air piracy became known as skyjacking, and it reached an apogee of sorts in the early 1970s.

One of the more notable skyjackings began on November 10, 1972, on board a Southern Airways DC-9 carrying 31 people from Birmingham to Montgomery, Alabama. A few minutes into the flight, three young men who were already in trouble with the law produced pistols and hand grenades and commandeered the plane. They demanded a $10 million ransom. "I'm not playing," one said. "If you do not get that money together, I'm gonna crash this plane in Oak Ridge"—the nuclear facility in Tennessee.

A mad 29-hour, 4,000-mile hopscotch ride to eight airports ensued, the crew growing ever wearier, the passengers ever more filled with dread. Southern Airways, a small outfit, managed to scrape together $2 million, which the hijackers took to Cuba. Unexpectedly, however, they got the deep freeze from Fidel Castro, who was having his own problems with skyjackers. Back they flew to Orlando, Florida, and talked irrationally about taking the short-range jet across the Atlantic to Switzerland.

On the tarmac, FBI agents tried to shoot out the jet's four main tires, but only flattened two. The gunmen "were raving maniacs after that," said a passenger. "Before, they were just docile maniacs." They shot and wounded the copilot and ordered the plane aloft once more. Captain William Haas coaxed the damaged jet into the air—then safely down onto a foam-covered runway, again in Havana. There the ordeal ended, with the Cubans marching the skyjackers off at gunpoint and cooperating in the return of plane, crew, passengers, and, later, the money.

In only 10 of the 31 skyjackings attempted in the United States that year did the perpetrator successfully control the flight and reach his destination. With improving security, the incidence of skyjackings declined as the decade progressed.

Southern Airways Flight 49 sits surrounded by fuel trucks on the tarmac at Toronto, Ontario, third stop on a wild November 1972 ride that included two landings in Cuba. Flight 49 skyjackers Melvin C. Cale, Henry D. Jackson Jr., and Louis Cale are shown at right with 18 other skyjackers of U.S. flights in 1972, along with their prison sentences or other outcomes.

Richard LaPoint
40 years

Garrett Trapnell
Life

Richard F. McCoy
45 years

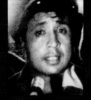
Stanley Speck
Psychiatric
commitment

Ricardo Chavez-Ortiz
Life

William H. Greene III
20 years

Robb Heady
30 years

Willie Roger Holder
Asylum—Algeria

Catherine Marie Kerkow
Asylum—Algeria

Martin J. McNally
Life

Dimitr Alexiev
Killed by FBI agents

Michael Azmanoff
Killed by FBI agents

Francis Michael
Goodell
30 years

Michael Stanley Green
50 years

Frank Markoe Sibley
Life

Charles A. Tuller
100 years

Bryce Tuller
100 years

Jonathan Tuller
100 years

Melvin C. Cale
15 years (in Cuba)

Henry D. Jackson Jr.
20 years (in Cuba)

Louis Cale
20 years (in Cuba)

A Despicable Killing Machine

Tall and handsome, young Theodore Robert Bundy impressed men and women active in Washington State politics with his can-do attitude and willingness to serve. He became so adept at ingratiating himself that law-and-order Republicans could imagine him one day running for governor. But behind Ted Bundy's charming smile lurked a monster *(inset)*, a hate-filled slaughterer of young women.

Born out of wedlock and raised by a tyrannical grandfather, Bundy was troubled even as a toddler; when he was three he started slipping butcher knives under the bedclothes of sleeping female relatives. As far as anyone knows, the stalking, abducting, raping, torturing, and killing began in 1973—just as he was making such a strong impression as a budding politico. His first victims were pretty young women who wore long hair parted in the middle—like a girl who had once spurned him.

Bundy killed at least 11 women in Washington and as many more in Utah and Colorado after moving to Salt Lake City in 1974. He was so good at covering up his crimes that it took police years to get the goods on him. Arrested for kidnapping in October 1975, he made bail but was eventually convicted. Later tried for murder, he escaped from jail twice, the second time making his way to Florida. There he rampaged through a Florida State University sorority house, killing two coeds and maiming others in just one night. His last victim was a 12-year-old girl.

Finally caught, tried, and convicted, he was sentenced to die in July 1979 but spent nine years on death row battling for his life before going to Florida's electric chair. Although he formally confessed to 30 murders, even Bundy couldn't keep his victims straight. "Terrible with names—and faces," he smirked. When a policeman suggested that he had killed 36 women, Bundy said, "Add one digit to that and you'll have it." Did he mean 37, or 136? No one would ever know.

Shackled in leg irons, serial murderer Ted Bundy pores over a law book in a Colorado courthouse, where he acted as his own attorney in 1977. Days later, he escaped through the ceiling of his prison cell and fled to Florida to kill again.

From Heiress to Terrorist: A Good Girl Gone Bad

On February 4, 1974, two men and a woman dragged a screaming, half-naked coed from an apartment near the University of California, in Berkeley, stuffed her into the trunk of a white convertible, sprayed the street with gunfire, and roared away. She was Patricia Hearst, 19-year-old granddaughter of fabled newspaper tycoon William Randolph Hearst. Her abductors styled themselves the Symbionese Liberation Army. Thus began a bizarre saga.

The SLA, an organization of a dozen or so militant radicals, instructed Patty's parents that to keep her alive they must distribute $6 million worth of food to San Francisco's needy. Patty sent a taped message saying she was okay, but pleading "I want to get out of here."

Over the following weeks the Hearsts received more tapes in the same vein. Then, on April 3, came the shocker: a recording in which Patty stated that she'd been given the choice of being released or joining the SLA's revolutionary struggle. "I have chosen to stay and fight," she declared, and condemned her family as "the pig Hearsts." Henceforth Patty would be freedom fighter Tania, and she sent a photo of herself wielding a carbine.

Twelve days later she appeared in another photo—this one taken by a San Francisco bank security camera—pointing a gun at customers while her comrades heisted $10,000. A month after that, Patty shot up a Los Angeles storefront to cover the escape of friends caught shoplifting. But the next day the SLA's spree abruptly ended. Six members died in a shootout with cops. Patty and two SLA comrades went on the run, staying hidden for 16 months. The FBI, after a nationwide manhunt, finally collared them in San Francisco on September 18, 1975.

At her trial for robbery, assault, and use of a firearm in the commission of a felony, Patty testified that her captors had first kept her drugged and blindfolded in a tiny closet and threatened to kill her, then brainwashed her. The jury didn't buy it. She was given seven years but served less than two before President Carter commuted her sentence in 1979.

Patty Hearst, as Tania the revolutionary, cradles her carbine before the seven-headed cobra banner affected by the Symbionese Liberation Army. Upon being arrested, she first gave her occupation as "urban guerrilla."

A "White Night" of Mass Death

It would be hard to say just when Jim Jones *(inset)* went mad; the dementia had been building for some time. Mesmerizing in the pulpit, the one-time Disciples of Christ minister found many Californians ready for his vision of a Christian-socialist paradise of racial harmony, common property, and good works. But followers at his San Francisco temple acknowledged that Jones was displaying certain quirks. He began referring to himself as Jesus Christ and demanding compliance with his every wish, including sexual favors and a flood of cash.

In 1974 part of Jones's flock traveled to Guyana, in South America, there to carve out a haven called Jonestown. Jones arrived in 1977, after reporters started looking into misuse of congregation funds. He worked his flock without mercy and punished slackers with floggings, electric shock, and confinement in boxes. After dark, he would make them practice a scenario he called White Night—a mass suicide symbolizing, he said, ultimate love and consent.

Eventually, word of the unholy doings got back to followers' relatives, and on November 17, 1978, California representative Leo Ryan, accompanied by newsmen, flew to Jonestown to investigate. As Ryan's party, along with 14 defectors, prepared to leave, some of Jones's henchmen, acting on his orders, opened fire, killing Ryan and four others.

That night became a White Night for real. Jones's lieutenants laced a tubful of fruit drink with cyanide and made the faithful drink up. Next day, Guyanese found 913 dead —among them Jones, a bullet in his head.

Looking from a distance like windblown laundry, hundreds of Jim Jones's followers lie dead in Guyana after drinking a poisoned fruit drink at his command. Those who balked at suicide were shot.

The Imam's Hostages

D eath to America! Death to the Great Satan!" howled the mob storming the U.S. embassy in Tehran on November 4, 1979. Soon 65 embassy staff were hostages of the Iranian Revolution (13 of these, women and blacks, were quickly released). Thus began one of the most humiliating and infuriating episodes in American history.

In 1953 the United States had been instrumental in restoring Iran's monarch, Mohammad Reza Shah Pahlavi, to the Peacock Throne of his ancestors, and it had long supported his regime as a stabilizing force in the Middle East. But the shah's secular, pro-Western policies, enforced brutally by his U.S.-trained secret police, had alienated his people.

In February 1979 a long-simmering fundamentalist Muslim revolt, led by a fierce old imam, Ruhollah Khomeini, forced the shah into exile. When the shah was later allowed into the United States for medical treatment, outraged Iranians demanded that he be given up for trial— and took the diplomats hostage to enforce their will.

For endless months to come, the American public would be subject- ed to nightly TV spectacles of rabid mobs in Tehran chanting hatred for the United States and burning the Stars and Stripes. The demoralizing ordeal worsened when a U.S. military mission to rescue the hostages on April 24, 1980, failed miserably and cost the lives of five men. The agony continued until Khomeini—after 444 days—freed the hostages the day Ronald Reagan succeeded Jimmy Carter as president.

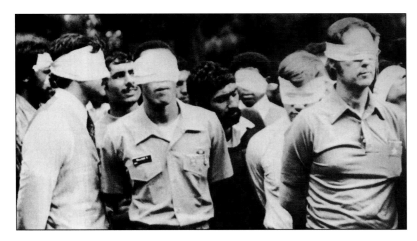

Iran's Ayatollah Khomeini (right), his malevolence captured by a Western photogra- pher, called his revolutionary reign "the government of God." Above, U.S. embassy personnel, bound and blindfolded, are paraded before jeering crowds.

Dress Rehearsal for Cataclysm

Critics of nuclear power had warned that a catastrophe somewhere was inevitable, and on March 30, 1979, their worst fears nearly came to pass. A reactor at Pennsylvania's Three Mile Island plant went sour. There had been troubles during the reactor's shakedown testing the year before, and engineers had questioned whether the power company and its technicians were familiar enough with the reactor to run it safely. But the company had hurried the plant into service to meet a deadline on tax credits and deductions. Now, a series of mechanical breakdowns and human blunders prompted a crisis. When a crucial water pump failed, backup systems were useless because workers had neglected to reopen valves they had closed for maintenance. That mistake was compounded by other system errors until the rapidly overheating uranium core approached meltdown.

Wisps of radioactive gas leaked into the atmosphere, and a huge hydrogen bubble began accumulating inside the damaged reactor, threatening to explode. After six frightening days, engineers managed to cool down the core and bleed off the gas bubble. There were no fatalities or cases of radiation poisoning, but the Nuclear Regulatory Commission conceded that, in addition to the company's errors, it had been ill prepared for the emergency and slow to react. Its people at the scene, for example, could report to Washington only via jammed telephone lines.

Reforms were instituted for the 72 U.S. plants in operation and the 124 on the way. Yet, as one observer said of Three Mile Island, "Those four huge cooling towers on the skyline will never look so innocent again."

Looming in the haze, the nuclear plant at Three Mile Island was predicted never to reopen after its partial meltdown in 1979, prompting Senator Gary Hart to call it "a billion-dollar mausoleum."

America Turns Inward

★

THE ME DECADE

Freewheeling, exotic, and self-absorbed, the 1970s lifestyle echoed many notes of the '60s counterculture but lacked its reforming energy. Americans' thoughts had turned from the public and social to the private and personal. The ideal way of life, as social critic Tom Wolfe put it in a famous magazine article in 1976 *(inset)*, had been transformed from changing society to "changing one's personality—remaking, remodeling, elevating, and polishing one's very self . . . and observing, studying, and doting on it."

By mid-decade, it seemed, the search for self had become obsessive. The media were rife with often-bizarre reports on the "human potential" movement—a catchall name for programs promising happiness, fulfillment, and union with the cosmos by means of anything from meditation to group "encounter sessions."

To accompany this new-style emotional self-improvement there was to be physical self-improvement. The '70s became the fitness decade, an earnest era that saw the popularization of health food and running.

Truly intense seekers found more direct routes to holiness: The '70s saw a religious revival embracing everything from Hindu disciplines to demented cults to charismatic Christianity. All advertised personal peace and some offered personal saviors. It was, after all—as Tom Wolfe so aptly put it—the Me Decade.

Under New Mexico skies Tom Law, a '70s dropout from urban "machine-soot vibrations," connects with the universe through yoga. "My head is in the stars," he says, "and yet I am here, too."

Seeking union with nature, clients at the Esalen Institute commune with the trees of California's Big Sur. Esalen, with its mix of New Age therapies, was home base for the human potential movement.

Los Angeles meditators hooked to biofeedback machines try to reach a state of conscious relaxation associated with alpha brain waves. Success was signaled by lights and musical tones.

Thomas A. Harris's bestseller (left) explained his pop psychology. Its quasi-religious message made it a hit with church groups.

An ecstatic Esalen client (opposite) enjoys the exercise known as group touching. The institute emphasized the importance of the mind-body connection and sensory awareness.

The Quest to Feel Best

Bewildered by the social changes of the '60s, disillusioned with traditional spiritual advice, many Americans in the 1970s went looking for happiness and security—for "self-knowledge," "individual transcendence," and "cosmic awareness." They found it in the wide array of programs aimed at maximizing "human potential." Mostly designed for groups, the programs seemed friendlier and less expensive than conventional psychotherapy. Almost everyone tried at least one of them, or knew someone who had: A 1976 Gallup poll tallied participants at 19 million.

Whatever they tried had probably appeared at least once at California's Esalen Institute. Everything from LSD to quantum physics to healing massage was explored there —"lube jobs for the personality," Tom Wolfe called them.

Many of the therapies derived from classical Asian meditation techniques, known for calming spirits and lowering blood pressure. Questers who had no time for classical training could find inner peace in 40 minutes a day by paying $125 for lessons in the transcendental meditation of the Maharishi Mahesh Yogi, an Indian guru who had 370 U.S. centers by 1975. For the science-minded there was biofeedback, with mechanically measured progress.

On the physical level were treatments based on holistic thinking, ranging from Gestalt therapy to the massage experience called rolfing. A program called Arica focused on dancing. Primal-scream therapy released rage.

Then there were quick-fix psychologies. The most famous was transactional analysis, embodied in a bestselling book *(left)*. It promised to teach people to behave like adults. Another was created by former salesman Jack Rosenberg, who, as Werner Erhard, began Erhard Seminar Training, or est. Est charged $250 for a weekend mental boot camp. Said Erhard, "I am here to explain what can't be explained." Est, like other therapies, made its inventor rich.

Exercising '70s style, runners pound down a Kansas street. Almost everyone could join in this sport: Six-year-old Bucky Cox (right) had completed his first marathon a few months before.

The Fitness Revolution

The exercise boom of the 1970s grew from many influences. For one thing, it was becoming clear that the major killer of Americans, heart disease, originated in bad diets and poor physical conditioning. For another, fat was unfashionable. Furthermore, the '70s ideals of personal wholeness integrated body and soul in a new version of the ancient Greek idea, expressed by the Roman commentator Juvenal, of *mens sana in corpore sano*—"a sound mind in a sound body." And finally, people who took up serious exercise, especially running, discovered the spiritual pleasure it offered and became ardent proselytizers.

Among them was editor Jim Fixx, who began running, lost 60 pounds, and acquired serenity, focus, and a "sense of quiet power." "It will show you how to become healthier and happier than you have ever imagined you could be," promised his 1977 book *(inset),* which sold 650,000 copies.

For fitness freaks, running provided the ultimate high—including the release of euphoria-inducing brain chemicals called endorphins and enkephalins—in a decade devoted to highs. And huge numbers achieved it: A poll in 1979 revealed that 40 million people—a fifth of the population— were running.

New Balance running shoes

Ingredients old and new became staples for healthful eaters. Left to right, top row: cranberry beans, unsulfurized apricots, toasted kasha; center row: nuts, black beans, adzuki beans, sunflower seeds; bottom row: millet, fava beans, red lentils.

Looking like prehistoric carvings, loaves such as these meant good eating in the health-conscious '70s: Not supermarket white bread or crisp, light French baguettes, but coarse, heavy breads of corn, sprouted wheat, or rye, flavored with nuts or seeds.

A Passion for Healthful Food

An overfed nation stuffed on fats, sugar, and junk foods laced with salt and unknown additives was not a pretty—or a healthy—sight. It certainly was not appropriate to the figure-conscious, health-conscious '70s.

Signs of change were everywhere. In the mid-1960s the nation had perhaps 500 health food stores; by 1972 the total had passed 3,000, and supermarket chains were introducing health food sections. Health food restaurants and juice bars mushroomed.

Reducing diets and philosophies—the grapefruit diet, the Scarsdale diet, the Stillman diet—proliferated. Vegetarianism was on the rise. Organic produce, grown without chemical fertilizers or pesticides, and organic meat, from animals untreated with hormones or antibiotics, cost about 30 percent more than other food, yet demand was high. Sales of bottled spring water shot up.

But while faith in new modes of diet was strong, hard information was sketchy. Certainly, people were better off not taking in pesticides with their food, but did organic fertilizers actually make a difference? Could vitamin supplements cure diseases? Could vitamin C cure the common cold?

Controversy over such questions would continue for years, as would diet fads. But the '70s food obsession educated a generation. Lighter, more healthful nutrition was a valuable legacy of the Me Decade.

Signs of eating for health included fresh juices offered at a Los Angeles natural-foods café (above) and three popular books (right). Adele Davis, the "high priestess of nutrition," made controversial claims for vitamin supplements; Nobel laureate Linus Pauling did the same for vitamin C. The vegetarian cookbook from Moosewood, the legendary counterculture restaurant in Ithaca, New York, inspired affection as well as good diet.

SIGNET • 451-E5379 • $1.75

Let's Eat Right To Keep Fit

Adelle Davis

Author of *Let's Cook It Right*, and *Let's Have Healthy Children*. A world famous nutritionist's bestselling guide to physical and emotional well-being through proper diet.

OVER 3 MILLION COPIES IN PRINT
NEWLY REVISED AND UPDATED

A Nobel Prize-winning scientist tells how you may avoid colds and improve your health

Vitamin C and the Common Cold
by **Linus Pauling**

Including two new chapters especially written for this edition in which Dr. Pauling responds to the controversy aroused by this international bestseller.

MOOSEWOOD COOKBOOK

By Mollie Katzen

Speaking in Korean at a 1975 rally, the Unification Church's Reverend Sun Myung Moon preaches his curious mix of Christianity, occultism, and electrical engineering to a crowd of mesmerized American youth. To his followers he was a messiah, to their parents an evil cult leader, and to the U.S. government a tax evader.

Members of the International Society for Krishna Consciousness drum, sing, and dance in a 1975 celebration of an ancient Hindu festival in San Francisco's Golden Gate Park. Founded in 1966, the society required its young members to be chaste, obedient vegetarians and to sell incense on the streets to raise money.

Reaching for the Spirit

In its quest for fulfillment, the '70s generation sought the spiritual as well as the therapeutic and the healthful, but it was not the Establishment they turned to. Defections from traditional religion were endemic.

The trend was toward eclectic mysticism, including even experimentation with astrology, the tarot, alchemy, and witchcraft. Historian Theodore Roszak observed, "Nobody who ever talked with a witch or walked with a zombie goes without an attentive audience these days." More thoughtful seekers turned to Asian religions—to Zen or Tibetan Buddhism—that portrayed a cosmos permeated by divine spirit and understood through study and meditation.

The fluid atmosphere left the young vulnerable to persuasive talkers, and cults flourished. Among them were the vastly rich Unification Church *(left, top)* and the Divine Light Mission with its "updated" Hinduism, whose members served in hospitals and prisons and tithed 10 percent of their income. The mendicants of the International Society for Krishna Consciousness *(left, bottom)* were fixtures on city streets and at airports. The Church of Scientology, controversial brainchild of science-fiction writer L. Ron Hubbard, was a fixture in the news.

Alienated youth also turned, if briefly, to evangelical Christianity. Dramatic conversions, fervid baptisms, and holy rock concerts attracted a good deal of media attention early in the decade.

The Jesus freaks, as they were called, vanished as rapidly as they had appeared. What replaced them, or perhaps absorbed them, was a charismatic, fundamentalist, conservative religious revival among college students and adults. By 1977, 70 million claimed to be born-again Christians. Tom Wolfe wrote, "We are now—in the Me Decade—seeing the upward roll of the third great religious wave in American history . . . the Third Great Awakening."

Wearing her religious allegiance for all to see, a young convert to the Jesus movement spreads her arms in ecstasy while awaiting an ocean baptism near Newport Beach, California, in 1971.

Celebration
of Superstardom

★

A DECADE OF MEMORABLE MOMENTS

Great moments are the golden currency of sport. Athletes might win praise for teamwork, consistency, guts, or sportsmanship, but what defines any contest is that glorious instant when there is nothing more to give—or to wish for. That time arrived for swimmer Mark Spitz at the 1972 Munich Olympics. The 22-year-old Californian had started posting world marks at 16, but he had much to prove: Favored for six golds at the 1968 games, he had bragged about his prowess but then proved a dismal flop. Chastened, in 1972 he said only, "I'll just swim my best." He then proceeded to set seven world records in seven freestyle, butterfly, and relay races. When asked if he felt vindicated, he said softly, "I am in a bit of a trance."

The same could not be said of Hank Aaron *(inset)*. For him, baseball had narrowed down to a grueling quest to break the lifetime home-run record set by the immortal Babe Ruth in the 1920s and '30s—a quest marred by hate mail and death threats. Undaunted, the Atlanta Braves' outfielder finally drew even with the beloved Babe at 714 home runs. And then on the evening of April 8, 1974, the nation watched as a pitcher tried to blow a fastball by him. Crack! Number 715. Aaron stood alone atop the pinnacle. "Thank God, it's over," he said, while the baseball world roared its acclaim for the greatest slugger ever.

Building speed and stamina, Mark Spitz practices for the 1972 Munich Olympics. Some swimmers shaved their heads and bodies seal slick; the confident Spitz let his hair grow long and gloried in his mustache.

A Bumper Crop for Cooperstown

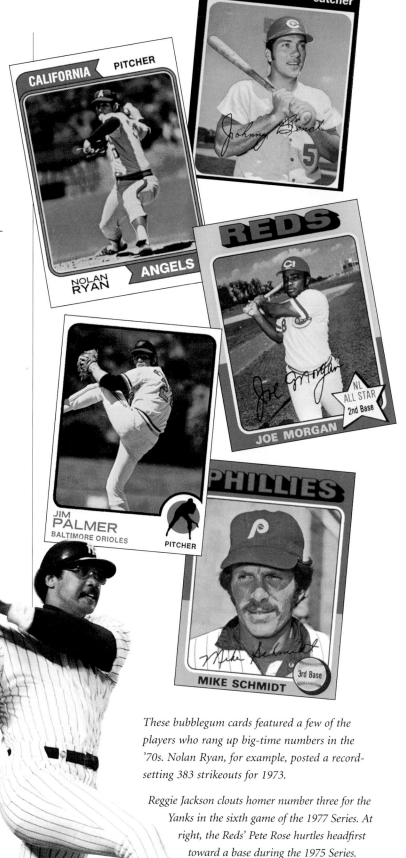

The superstars on these pages lent a special grace to baseball in the 1970s as they and a host of other great players carved out careers worthy of the Hall of Fame. Several of them had the good fortune to play on a team—there was one in each league—so loaded with talent that it created a minidynasty during the decade.

The Oakland Athletics might have gone down as the flakes of baseball. Under the stewardship of their prickly and unorthodox owner, businessman Charlie Finley, they wore zany green-and-gold uniforms, sprouted curlicue mustaches, and feuded bitterly with each other in the clubhouse. But they had the hitting, pitching, and glovework to dominate the American League and superslugger Reggie Jackson to lift them above themselves.

Brash and boisterous, a ladies' man, Jackson liked to say, "I'd rather hit than have sex." After helping the A's to three consecutive World titles (1972-1974), Jackson moved on to the New York Yankees, where he gained the nickname Mr. October for his record of postseason heroics and particularly for blasting three homers in one game as the Yanks beat the Dodgers four games to two in the 1977 Series.

The National League's powerhouse was the Cincinnati Reds, who won the pennant four times and the World Series in '75 and '76. In a Reds lineup rich with all-stars, leadoff hitter and third baseman Pete Rose set an example of never-say-die effort. Nicknamed Charlie Hustle, Rose once said, "I'd walk through hell in a gasoline suit just to play baseball." When *Sports Illustrated* named him Sportsman of the Year in 1975, it was, the magazine said, for "the sheer force of his personality."

These bubblegum cards featured a few of the players who rang up big-time numbers in the '70s. Nolan Ryan, for example, posted a record-setting 383 strikeouts for 1973.

Reggie Jackson clouts homer number three for the Yanks in the sixth game of the 1977 Series. At right, the Reds' Pete Rose hurtles headfirst toward a base during the 1975 Series.

Kareem Abdul-Jabbar of the Milwaukee Bucks, shooting his patented "skyhook," arcs the ball so high even the Lakers' seven-foot-two-inch Wilt Chamberlain can do nothing about it.

Applying a bit of elbow, the New York Knicks' Walt Frazier drives past an opponent. On and off the court, Frazier led the league in "cool."

Soaring Stars With Soaring Salaries

Parity was the name of the National Basketball Association's game in the 1970s. The New York Knicks and the Boston Celtics each won two NBA titles during the decade, but otherwise it was share the wealth. Six different teams, including the 1977-1978 Washington Bullets *(inset)*, collected championship rings.

For a while, the NBA faced competition from an upstart American Basketball Association, which featured a crowd-pleasing go-go game played with a startling red-white-and-blue ball. But the ABA got little coverage on TV, where the money lay, and in 1976 gave up the ghost. By then CBS-TV was paying the NBA $74 million a year for broadcast rights. And with that kind of loot going around, annual player salaries jumped to an average of $165,000 by decade's end.

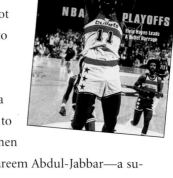

The Knicks, led by their great playmaker Walt Frazier, got where they were going with a rock-solid team effort, but most clubs looked to superstars for fan appeal. In Milwaukee and then LA, one such star was Lew Alcindor—later Kareem Abdul-Jabbar—a superbly coordinated seven-footer whose high-flying hook shot was unstoppable. After being named Rookie of the Year in 1970, Jabbar was voted Most Valuable Player three times in the next six seasons. "Who stops him?" an opposing coach once said. "No man alive. You just pray."

Sometimes a superstar is so vital to a team that he is called "the Franchise." For the ABA, Julius Erving was "the League." Erving, rated by many as the most exciting player of his day, had huge hands, steel-spring legs, and a genius for creativity. Nicknamed Dr. J for the way he "operated" on the court, Erving could score any way he wished, but his trademark play was a soaring, one-handed slam dunk. Averaging 31-plus points a game and leading his New York Nets to a pair of ABA titles, he helped keep the fledgling league alive as long as possible while creating a dazzling new offensive style that transformed all of basketball. When the ABA went under, the NBA absorbed the Nets and three other franchises—in the process snagging the inestimable Dr. J.

Outjumping everyone in sight, Julius "Dr. J" Erving of the ABA's New York Nets finishes off one of his spectacularly crowd-pleasing slam dunks.

Football Juggernaut's "Immaculate" Birth

It was one of those moments that change everything. With just 22 seconds left in a 1972 American Football Conference playoff semifinal, the Pittsburgh Steelers trailed the Oakland Raiders 7-6. Facing fourth down and a mile to go on his 40-yard line, Steelers quarterback Terry Bradshaw dropped back and threw. Defender, receiver, and pass came together in a split-second collision, the ball caroming harmlessly away—and that was the game, and Pittsburgh's season.

But no. As the ball plummeted toward the ground, rookie Steelers running back Franco Harris somehow scooped it off his shoetops and galloped 42 yards to the Raiders' end zone. Officials ruled that the intended receiver had never touched the ball and Harris's catch was thus legal. Sportswriters, taking their cue from the official call, dubbed the miracle touchdown play "the immaculate reception."

That was the first postseason victory in the Steelers'

woeful 40-year history. And it led coach Chuck Noll to remark, "Up until that point, I was the only one who believed that this was a good football team." Now, he said, the Steelers had become "a team of destiny."

From that time on Pittsburgh dominated the decade like no other team in sport. From 1972 to 1979 Chuck Noll's men won six division titles and became the first team in history to capture four Super Bowls, with back-to-back wins in 1975-1976 and 1979-1980. "We got the wheels in motion and made winning a perpetual thing," said Pittsburgh's fearsome defensive tackle, "Mean Joe" Greene, adding in a devilishly enigmatic epigram, "We learned that the more you win, the harder it is to lose."

Defeating Dallas 35-31 in the 1979 Super Bowl, Bradshaw passed for a record four touchdowns and 318 yards; many observers considered those '78 Steelers the greatest team in history. Miami fans demurred; for them—if for them alone—that honor goes to the 1972 Dolphins, who roared through the regular season, the playoffs, and the Super Bowl undefeated *(inset)*, the only team in league history to do so.

Toothless Jack Lambert and Mean Joe Greene apply the defensive crunch to an Oakland back. Joked Green to Bradshaw before the 1975 Super Bowl win over Minnesota, "Just hold 'em. We'll get the points."

A bevy of Steeler Super Bowl MVPs: Terry Bradshaw (near right) received the honor in both the third and fourth of Pittsburgh's championships. Franco Harris (center) broke records for carries and yards gained in the '75 game. Lynn Swann (far right) got up from a hospital bed to play and earn the award in '76.

More Jewels for Sport's Crown

For Americans, the 1970s offered more to cheer about in more different kinds of sports than in any previous era. The emergence of TV as a national, even worldwide spotlight for all manner of athletes undoubtedly had much to do with it, as did the caliber of the young competitors and the skyrocketing, million-dollar rewards being offered for athletic prowess. Ever since English runner Roger Bannister shattered the age-old barrier of the four-minute mile in 1954, it seemed the natural order of things that each new generation of athletes was bigger, stronger, faster, and more skilled than any that came before. The '70s put an exclamation point on the trend.

The Best Golfer Who Ever Lived

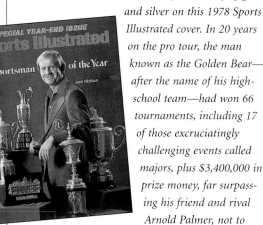

Beaming over the latest of his many honors, Jack Nicklaus stands surrounded by a treasury of gold and silver on this 1978 Sports Illustrated cover. In 20 years on the pro tour, the man known as the Golden Bear— after the name of his high-school team—had won 66 tournaments, including 17 of those excruciatingly challenging events called majors, plus $3,400,000 in prize money, far surpassing his friend and rival Arnold Palmer, not to mention such legends as Bobby Jones, Ben Hogan, and Sam Snead.

Gutsy, Graceful, Golden

Dazzling Dorothy Hamill slices through the air during a practice session before traveling to Innsbruck, Austria, for the 1976 Winter Olympics. Though plagued by precompetition jitters, the 19-year-old was the class of the field once she took to the ice, skating off with a gold medal for herself and the U.S. Later that year, she won the world championships at Göteborg, Sweden, and then began a stellar pro career, by which time her distinctive hairdo—fashioned by a New York stylist to fall back into place after every jump—was being copied by young women across the country.

Altercation in Africa

The referee tolls the count over a prostrate George Foreman while Muhammad Ali retires to a neutral corner at the climax of their October 1974 heavyweight championship fight in Kinshasa, Zaire. "The Rumble in the Jungle," as the ever poetic Ali termed it, not only won him back his crown but introduced a new "rope-a-dope" style. Instead of mixing it up midring, he lay back on the ropes, blocking the younger man's best shots while occasionally popping him one. By round five, Foreman was arm weary; in round eight, the 32-year-old Ali sent him down with a thunderous combination.

Wimbledon Royalty

Like any two lovebirds engaged to be married, tennis stars Chris Evert, 19, and Jimmy Connors, 21, smile happily for the camera in July 1974. The silverware was their reward (plus $40,800 and a sports car each) for brilliant victories in singles at Wimbledon. It was hard to say which of the two more thoroughly dominated the game during that heady year. With a blazing two-fisted backhand, Evert won 16 of 23 tournaments and $261,460 in prize money; Connors took 14 of 20 events, winning an unsurpassed $281,309. But 1975 was another year altogether; their romance cooled, as did their tennis. Evert lost in the semis at Wimbledon, and Connors was routed in the finals by the highly popular 32-year-old Arthur Ashe (below), who after 15 years in the big time finally realized all of his huge potential, becoming the first black male ever to capture that holiest of tennis grails.

A Champion 10 Times Over

America's Bruce Jenner exults after completing the 1,500-meter run, the final event of the decathlon at the 1976 Montreal Olympics. In this most punishing of contests, Jenner posted personal bests in eight of the 10 events to win the gold medal with a world record of 8,618 points. Anticipating an avalanche of commercial offers in case he succeeded, the movie-star-handsome young athlete had arranged for management help even before the games began; sure enough, shortly after his victory he found himself well on his way to an annual income in excess of half a million dollars.

Outrunning History

Jockey Ron Turcotte permits himself the luxury of a backward look at the distant field as the nonpareil thoroughbred Secretariat wins the 1973 Belmont Stakes by an incredible 31 lengths. That victory made the three-year-old colt the first winner of horse racing's fabled Triple Crown (the Kentucky Derby, the Preakness, and the Belmont) in 25 years. Yet the distinction did not last long: In a vintage decade for the sport of kings, Seattle Slew won the Triple Crown in 1977 and Affirmed did it again the very next year. Nevertheless, no horse ever touched Secretariat's 1:59.2 record for the one-and-a-quarter-mile Derby or his 2:24 record for the one-and-a-half-mile Belmont, times that would rank the Virginia-bred stallion as the greatest racehorse in history.

TV's Uneven Revolution

★

Television in the 1970s, especially sitcoms, brought the '60s revolution into the living room. The previous decade's big issues—race relations, the sexual revolution, and the antiwar movement—migrated off the streets and out of the evening news into family programming, changing prime time forever. Suddenly, characters of every hue, social class, and point of view were marching across the small screen in the name of entertainment.

Shows that included the formerly taboo subjects of sex and race topped the charts. *Roots (right)*, Alex Haley's saga of his own African American family, smashed the color barrier in January 1977 and, with an estimated 130 million viewers, broke almost every ratings record in TV history. Two hundred years after Haley's ancestor Kunta Kinte was abducted from his African village, viewers tuned in for 12 hours over eight nights, engrossed in the story.

Prime-time sex was more complex. The '70s were a time of heightened sensibilities among women, yet most TV executives found "sexy" more appealing than "feminist." The women's liberation movement as viewed through the leering lens of TV revealed tough but shapely heroines like *Charlie's Angels (inset),* seductively dressed detectives who started beating up bad guys in 1976. The beautiful threesome, played by Jaclyn Smith, Kate Jackson, and Farrah Fawcett-Majors, may actually have been a

African American life, formerly given little attention on TV, broke through in the 1970s. Roots (right) portrayed the horrors of slavery and, coincidentally, boosted the popularity of the miniseries genre.

Funny lady Carol Burnett hams it up as a char-woman, one of her many memorable characters on the long-running Carol Burnett Show. A stalwart of CBS's prime-time lineup from 1967 to 1978, it was one of the last variety shows.

Kermit the Frog shares a moment with Miss Piggy on The Muppet Show, a combination of comedy and music that premiered in 1976. Jim Henson's puppets were joined each week by a guest celebrity.

backlash against feminism. In any case, the sex-fantasy series made a big splash with male viewers, while some women, at least, identified with the Angels' assertiveness, spirit of adventure, and self-confidence.

Mary Richards, heroine of *The Mary Tyler Moore Show (page 172)*, won sympathy and laughs with her struggles to "make it on her own." Like an increasing number of female viewers, she was a newly liberated career woman. Starting in 1970 she turned "the world on with her smile," aided by her outspoken pal, Rhoda; her gruff boss at the WJM newsroom, Lou Grant; and Ted Baxter, the idiotically narcissistic anchorman.

In January 1971 CBS nervously premiered a sitcom so certain to spark controversy that the network warned viewers: "The program you are about to see is *All in the Family.* It seeks to throw a humorous spotlight on our frailties, prejudices, and concerns."

Controversial it was, but *All in the Family* not only became a smash hit, it also altered the course of television comedy. For the first time, a sitcom played bigotry and politics for laughs. Big-mouthed grouch Archie Bunker had black neighbors, a feminist daughter, a leftist son-in-law, and a tendency to blat ethnic or sexual slurs. Archie and his simpleminded but sweet wife, Edith (whom he often called Dingbat), their daughter, Gloria, and son-in-law, Mike (aka Meathead), took on abortion, homosexuality, and menopause. "If you're going to have your change of life, have it right now!" shouted Archie at Edith. "You've got exactly 30 seconds!" Mike and Archie argued over Watergate just weeks after the real events; conversations were punctuated by the hilariously timed flush of the upstairs toilet. There was even an episode in which Edith was attacked by a rapist—the realism added substance to the humor.

Because *All in the Family* was recorded live on videotape, it *felt* real, too. If it mirrored Americans' prejudices, said Norman Lear, the show's co-creator, it also gave viewers permission to laugh while "swallowing the littlest bit of truth" about themselves.

The laughter continued with later Lear shows. *Sanford and Son* (1972) focused on a black father-and-son junk dealership in the Los Angeles inner city *(page 172)*. *Maude* (1972) was an *All in the Family* spin-off about Edith's militantly liberal and opinionated cousin. *Good Times* (1974), a spin-off of a spin-off, presented the adventures of Maude's black maid, Florida Evans, who moved to Chicago with her complicated family. *The Jeffersons* (1975), another *All in the Family* spin-off, featured the Bunkers' middle-class black neighbors.

Other sitcoms added new colors to the cultural rainbow. *Chico and the*

An American comedy with bite: All in the Family's inimitable Archie Bunker (Carroll O'Connor) poses with wife, Edith (Jean Stapleton), daughter, Gloria (Sally Struthers), and son-in-law, Mike (Rob Reiner). The groundbreaking, highly popular sitcom was the first to deal openly with hot issues of prejudice, politics, and sex.

Man (1974) told the tale of Mexican American characters in a rundown garage in East Los Angeles. *Taxi* (1978-1983) went behind the scenes of a New York cab company with an ethnically diverse fraternity of wacko drivers and dreamers.

When it came to mixing drama with comedy, none of the '70s sitcoms rivaled *M*A*S*H*. An adaptation of a 1970 Korean War film, the show cut to the bone of fear and friendship, love and loneliness, horror and heroism among army doctors, nurses, and GIs. Surgeon Hawkeye (Alan Alda) guzzled home-distilled gin and used scalpel-sharp wit to mock army regulations and uptight attitudes while applying deep compassion to his compatriots' and patients' emotional wounds. *M*A*S*H* acknowledged indirectly the cultural anguish and confusion created by American involvement in the Vietnam War. The humor was often dark, and the laughs all the stronger for it.

Worlds apart in setting and attitude, the humor of *The Waltons* was homespun and heartfelt. Set in rural Virginia during the Depression, the saga of the Walton family, as told by eldest son John-Boy, was fraught with love, death, and sibling squabbles. Soothing, if a tad syrupy—episodes ended with family members calling out good-night to each other—*The Waltons* was the first family-drama series of the '70s.

Programs like *The Waltons* fit right into the "family hour" instituted by the networks in mid-decade to appease critics of increasing sex and violence on TV. Between 8:00 and 9:00 p.m. other new dramas featured such courageous families as the Ingallses of

The Waltons
(1972-1981)

Sanford and Son
(1972-1977)

The Mary Tyler Moore Show
(1970-1977)

Taxi
(1978-1983)

The staff of the 4077th Mobile Army Surgical Hospital—or M*A*S*H—entertained viewers with sophisticated, and often black, humor for 11 years.

When tough-talking, hot-tempered Lieutenant Theo Kojak said, "Who loves ya, baby?" viewers knew that some character had won his approval. Telly Savalas played the dapper New York City cop who fought crime in the streets. Controversial for its high quotient of violence, the program nevertheless attracted a wide audience.

Stripped for action, Wonder Woman Diana Prince, as played by Lynda Carter, stands ready to fight crime. Although her story was originally set in the 1940s, the female superhero gave '70s feminists much to cheer about. Indeed, Carter, a former ballet student and champion swimmer, performed many of her own stunts.

"Good evening. I'm Chevy Chase and you're not. Our top story tonight. . ."

Saturday Night Live's "Weekend Update" anchor Chevy Chase

Little House on the Prairie. Ma, Pa, Laura, and her sisters settled down on a prime-time homestead in 1974 and rose to the top of the charts.

The new programming requirements encouraged a crop of adventure-fantasy series, such as The Six Million Dollar Man (1973), starring Lee Majors as cybernetic astronaut Steve Austin, and The Bionic Woman (1976), with Lindsay Wagner as his technologically improved Adam's rib.

Sex and violence were wedged into the 9:00-11:00 p.m. slot—dubbed Slime at Nine by one critic. Kojak (1973) led the array of gritty new urban crime dramas. Telly Savalas's strong role as the bald, lollipop-sucking detective turned the charismatic Greek American actor into an unlikely sex symbol. And where violence lurked, sex soon followed, in the curvaceous form of Wonder Woman. Lynda Carter, playing comic-book-derived Diana Prince, offered fantasy with a feminist twist: a superheroine who fought evil and looked good doing it. Wonder Woman joined Charlie's Angels in heralding a new genre of "jiggle" shows. Another was Three's Company (1977), in which Suzanne Somers and Joyce DeWitt wriggled and giggled around their apartment with pretend-gay roommate John Ritter.

A new TV form, late-night television comedy, was born when Saturday Night Live hit the airwaves in 1975. SNL and its wacky troupe of young performers, the "Not Ready for Prime Time Players," raised irreverence and disregard for convention to new heights while breaking every ratings mark for its slot.

In 1979 reality—as opposed to realism—got a firm foothold on late-night TV with the Iran hostage crisis. What began on ABC as a special nightly 15-minute update on the situation became ABC News Nightline, a permanent news program that kept running after the crisis ended. Viewers got into the habit of tuning in every night after the late news as the earnest young Ted Koppel narrated America's real real-life drama.

Unforgettable Oddballs From *SNL*

"Live, from New York, it's Saturday Night!" Saturday Night Live emerged as the most daring show of the late '70s. Deliberately outrageous and occasionally tasteless, it ran regular segments featuring such zany characters as the Coneheads (above) from "France"—actually from the planet Remulak—played by Dan Aykroyd, Jane Curtin, and Laraine Newman. Gilda Radner as Weekend Update's consumer reporter, Roseanne Roseannadanna (below), was obsessed with belly-button lint, while John Belushi's pseudo-Japanese-spouting samurai shopkeeper (right) sliced through objects at the drop of a sword.

The Decade
of the Director

★

"A GOLDEN AGE OF FILMMAKING"

George, Marty, Francis, and I . . . It was a golden age of filmmaking because we were all single, ambitious, and we were in love with film." So said Steven Spielberg about George Lucas, Martin Scorsese, and Francis Ford Coppola, rightfully including himself in the quartet of directors who redefined moviemaking in the 1970s with such films as *Jaws* and *Taxi Driver (inset)*. Unlike their predecessors who had been trained on studio back lots, this new breed of director had learned their craft in film schools. Knowledge of the history and theory of film imbued their moviemaking with a more personal narrative and visual style.

Hollywood old-timers may have sniffed at these "film-school brats," but young film fans responded with enthusiasm. That the director, not the writer or producer, was the real author of a movie was a new notion to be sure, yet the smartest of the studio heads were inclined to listen to the click-click-click of the turnstiles.

The result was the decade of the director, a new Hollywood era of youth, personal style, and experimentation, punctuated by works that expanded the horizons of film. Francis Ford Coppola, who had first gained recognition with the low-budget, modestly successful 1967 picture *You're a Big Boy Now*,

As Mafia boss Don Vito Corleone, Marlon Brando listens gravely to an associate in The Godfather. The 1972 film won Academy Awards for best picture and best screenplay. Brando was named best actor.

The evil Galactic Empire's Darth Vader looms overhead as rebels Han Solo (Harrison Ford), Luke Skywalker (Mark Hamill), and Princess Leia (Carrie Fisher) blaze away in this poster (above, top) for Star Wars. Merchandising of everything from T-shirts to buttons added millions to the profits. Above, this still of a Rebel fighter swerving to evade attack exemplifies the movie's high-tech visuals.

was only 33 years old in 1972 when he put Mario Puzo's *The Godfather (page 177)* on the screen. About as different from the basic gangster flick as a .44 magnum is from a cap pistol, *The Godfather* omitted not one measure of the operatic highs and lows of the cruel, complex, oddly corporate mafioso life—and enriched Paramount by $86 million, nearly double the money made by any of its previous hits. Even that sum looked puny three years later when Steven Spielberg, just 27, infused Peter Benchley's novel *Jaws* with such realistic horror that the shark-eats-man drama brought Universal a staggering $130 million.

Native New Yorker Martin Scorsese, born in 1942, explored the underside of life in his hometown with *Mean Streets* (1973), a look at young mobsters-to-be, and *Taxi Driver* (1976), a chilling portrait of a psychotic Vietnam veteran. Although too intense for widespread box-office appeal, such works catapulted Scorsese into the ranks of the boldest of the new breed.

But the triumph of the decade belonged to George Lucas, who first became known in 1973 for *American Graffiti,* which portrayed the rites of teenage passage in small-town America. Despite the success of *Graffiti,* Lucas was getting nowhere with a favorite idea: a space saga called *Star Wars.*

Eventually, 20th Century-Fox came up with $9.5 million—enough for Lucas to fabricate a fantasy universe of good and evil, rebels and tyrants, knights and princesses, pilots and droids, all doing battle in outer space. For visuals, Lucas founded a new kind of Hollywood enterprise, Industrial Light and Magic—and it was magic his wizards created, electronically blending light, movement, and images to give birth to a new genre of special-effects movies.

As a youngster, Lucas had been enraptured by adventure movies and comic books, and through his cherished space epic he shared his delight in those childhood pleasures. "My main reason for making *Star Wars,*" he said, "was to give young people an honest, wholesome fantasy life, the kind my generation had." And the kid in everyone turned it into the blockbuster of the decade, with $460 million in receipts.

Heroes in their own right, droids C-3PO and R2-D2 confer on strategy against villain Darth Vader's juggernaut. Looking like a futuristic vacuum cleaner (but with a real-live, three-foot eight-inch actor inside), gutsy little R2-D2 proved instrumental in vaporizing the empire's seemingly invulnerable Death Star.

A Decade of Icons

"G o ahead, make my day," rasped Clint Eastwood as the blow-'em-away 1970s police detective "Dirty Harry" Callahan. The characterization violated the norms of cops-and-robbers films, but it was the sort of sensational, audience-provoking approach that turned Eastwood and a company of other actors into powerful presences on the screen.

The new Hollywood of pioneering directors was made to order for young male actors portraying antiheroes at odds with convention, with the establishment, with themselves, with everything. Robert De Niro plumbed the depths of alienation as the obsessive urban vigilante in *Taxi Driver.* Jack Nicholson, Al Pacino, Dustin Hoffman, and Sylvester Stallone burned with intensity and conviction, bringing their own gritty realism to the screen. Less intense, except in sex appeal, was Robert Redford in such hits as *Jeremiah Johnson, The Sting,* and *All the President's Men.*

Clint Eastwood as Dirty Harry

On the wrong side of the fence in 1975's One Flew Over the Cuckoo's Nest, Jack Nicholson starred as the rebellious rogue who feigns insanity to avoid a prison stretch; the mental ward he is sent to destroys him when he tries to buck its system. Cuckoo won the academy's big five: best picture, actor, actress, director, and screenplay.

Washington Post investigative reporters Carl Bernstein (Dustin Hoffman, far left) and Bob Woodward (Robert Redford) break the Watergate scandal in 1976's All the President's Men. Hoffman's enormous range brought him roles in the 1970s as a harried single father, a smut-mouthed comic, a milquetoast husband, and a 121-year-old adoptive Indian.

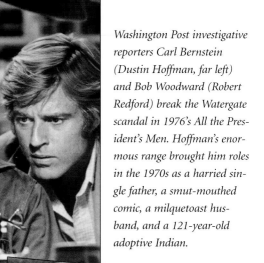

As an undercover cop in 1973's Serpico, Al Pacino wore beads, fringe, long hair, and beard while battling New York City police corruption. An acclaimed stage actor with Obie and Tony awards to his credit, Pacino first made it big in Hollywood alongside Marlon Brando in The Godfather, playing Don Corleone's favorite son and heir.

Battered but unbowed, Sylvester Stallone as Rocky Balboa, a stumblebum boxer and loan shark's enforcer, is embraced after improbably giving the heavyweight champ the fight of his life. Critics sneered at Stallone's script, but audiences stood up and cheered. "Rocky was never about boxing. It was always about a man simply fighting for his dignity," said Stallone upon the film's winning the 1976 Oscar for best picture.

Women Take Charge

Movie roles for women in the 1970s reflected the changing way women were looking at themselves and what they wanted from life. Hollywood leading ladies got more from their careers than steamy sexpot or virginal pretty-face roles.

There was still plenty of room for romance, but Hollywood began to pay attention to the three-dimensional conflicts and choices actually faced by women in their lives. Even the musical developed a distinct edge. *Cabaret,* for example, was searing testimony to the creative decadence of 1920s Berlin before the rise of Adolf Hitler tore it all asunder. Stage center was Liza Minnelli, who gave an Oscar-winning performance as a pregnant singer and dancer deciding not to have her child, partly because of an unfulfilling relationship with its bisexual father and partly because it would interfere with her show business career. Not noble, certainly, but sometimes life was like that.

Liza Minnelli in *Cabaret*

Jane Fonda underwent a transformation from sex kitten to feminist role model as the introspective call girl (right) struggling to come to terms with herself in 1971's Klute, for which she won an Oscar. Fonda won a second Oscar for her portrayal of a dutiful but repressed wife in the 1978 post-Vietnam flick Coming Home.

Playing a lady with a dark and secret past, Faye Dunaway draws a bead on her domineering, incestuous father in Chinatown, a mix of politics and murder in a corrupt Los Angeles of the 1930s. The 1974 thriller earned her an Oscar nomination; the award itself came two years later for her role as a ratings-obsessed TV producer in Network.

Discovering her social conscience, a blazing-eyed Sally Field lays into the union-busting bosses of a southern textile mill in 1979's Norma Rae. Until then, Field had been known mainly as TV's Flying Nun and was in danger of being pigeonholed as an actress of little consequence. "I needed the part," she said. "I was a cartoon."

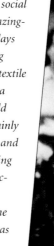

A blissful Barbra Streisand gazes aloft after making love to heart-throb Robert Redford in *The Way We Were*. Pairing 1973's top stars in an old-fashioned love story spelled box-office success.

A Medley of Memories

This gallery of movie posters from the 1970s includes Shaft, which pioneered the blaxploitation genre of films made by and for African Americans; the sci-fi thriller Alien; the gory hit The Exorcist; the funny but raunchy Blazing Saddles; and the slick dance musical Grease.

ACKNOWLEDGMENTS

The editors wish to thank the following individuals and institutions for their valuable assistance in the preparation of this volume:

Richard Allen, Lynden, Wash.; Judy and Ed Ashley, Jed Collectibles, Pemberton, N.J.; James Beck, A.J.'s Sport Stop, Vienna, Va.; Tom Conroy, Movie Still Archives, Harrison, Nebr.; Lawson Desrochers, NFL Properties, Inc., Los Angeles; Jeff Elmendorf, Funk & Junk, Alexandria, Va.; Erin Hogan, Rock and Roll Hall of Fame and Museum, Cleveland; Mary Ison and staff, Library of Congress, Washington, D.C.; Jim Marshall, San Francisco; Raegan Marshall, Universal Press Syndicate, Kansas City, Mo.; Milo Stewart Jr., National Baseball Hall of Fame; Cooperstown, N.Y.

PICTURE CREDITS

The sources for the illustrations in this book appear below. Credits from left to right are separated by semicolons, from top to bottom by dashes.
Cover and dust jacket: J.-P. Laffont/Sygma, New York (2); Photofest, New York (2); © 1976 Alex Webb/Magnum Photos, Inc., New York; UPI/Corbis-Bettmann; Everett Collection, New York—AP/Wide World Photos.
3: Courtesy Antonio Alcalá. **6, 7**: Michael Mauney, *Life* Magazine © Time Inc. Reprinted with permission; Hubert Van Es-UPI/Corbis-Bettmann. **8, 9**: Jerome Brent. **10, 11**: Stanley J. Forman, *Boston Herald*, Pulitzer Prize Spot News, 1977. **12, 13**: Martin Rogers, Irving, Tex. **14, 15**: Robin Platzer/Twin Images, New York. **16, 17**: Gary Settle/NYT Permissions. **18, 19**: Douglas Kirkland. **20, 21**: Eugene Cernan/NASA. **22**: William Sievert, Rehoboth Beach, Del.—Howard Ruffner. **23**: UPI/Corbis-Bettmann, *Life* Magazine © Time Inc. Reprinted with permission; DOONESBURY © 1970 G. B. Trudeau. Reprinted with permission of UNIVERSAL PRESS SYNDICATE. All rights reserved—private collection; © Time Inc. Reprinted by permission. **24**: Movie Still Archives, Harrison, Nebr. **25**: National Archives Neg. No. 8528#2; Frederick Stires—Stanley Tretick/Sygma, New York, *Life* Magazine © Time Inc. Reprinted with permission; Stern/Black Star, New York—Movie Still Archives, Harrison, Nebr. **27**: UPI/Corbis-Bettmann—© Time Inc. Reprinted by permission; Cheetham/Magnum Photos, Inc., New York; Alex Webb/Magnum Photos, Inc., New York. **28**: David Hume Kennerly—Bruce McBroom/Globe Photos, New York. **29**: Martha Swope; Elizabeth Sunflower/Pledge, New York; J. S. Attinello/Photri-Microstock, Falls Church, Va. **30**: Mark Godfrey, The Image Works, Woodstock, N.Y.—© Time Inc. Reprinted by permission. **31**: Fred Maroon, Washington, D.C.—NASA; John Frost Historical Newspaper Service, New Barnet, Hertfordshire/copyright Associated Newspapers Group, London. **32**: N. W. Owen/Black Star, New York—Jay Ullal/Stern/Black Star, New York. **33**: Movie Still Archives, Harrison, Nebr.; William Sievert, Rehoboth Beach, Del.—Elliott Erwitt/Magnum Photos, Inc., New York; Ledru/Sygma, New York. **34, 35**: Philippe Halsman © Halsman Estate. **36, 37**: Official White House Photo. **39**: Bruce Talamon, Los Angeles, Calif. **40, 41**: Bill Ray/*Life* Magazine © Time Inc. **43**: Frank Cowan/*Life* Magazine. **45**: UPI/Corbis-Bettmann. **46, 47**: Stanley Tretick/Sygma, New York. **49**: Michael Mauney/*Life* Magazine. **50, 51**: National Archives Neg. No. 2860-1. **52**: © 1972 Time Inc. Reprinted by permission—© 1972 Magnum/Magnum Photos, Inc., New York. **53**: Photograph by Harry Benson. **54, 55**: Private collection (3); Richard Swanson, *Life* Magazine © Time Inc.—photograph by Harry Benson. **56, 57**: AP/Wide World Photos (5); Dennis Brack Ltd./Black Star, New York—Stan Wayman/*Life* Magazine; James Worrell, New York (7). **58**: National Archives Neg. No. 624.217—© 1972 *The Washington Post*. Reprinted with permission; AP/Wide World Photos. **59**: UPI/Corbis-Bettmann. **60, 61**: Gjon Mili, *Life* Magazine © Time Inc. **62, 63**: Fred Ward Prod., Inc./Black Star, New York; © J.-P. Laffont/Sygma, New York; Fred Maroon, Washington, D.C.—Gjon Mili, *Life* Magazine © Time Inc. **64**: Dennis Brack Ltd./Black Star, New York. **65**: UPI/Corbis-Bettmann; © 1973 The New York Times Co. Reprinted with permission—National Archives Neg. No. WPO#E1874-4A-5. **66, 67**: Photograph by Harry Benson; National Archives. **68, 69**: Mark Jury, Dalton, Pa.; Koichiro Morita-AP/Wide World Photos/*Life* Magazine © Time Inc. Reprinted with permission. **70, 71**: John P. Filo, East Windsor, N.J.; John A. Darnell Jr./*Life* Magazine. **72**: Henri Huet/Associated Press, London—© George Butler, New York. **73**: Don McCullin, London. **74**: David Hume Kennerly—© Jerry Gay, Seattle, Wash. **75**: © 1977 Robin Hood. **76**: Nick Ut-AP/Wide World Photos. **77**: Photograph by Harry Benson. **78**: Gamma Liaison/Liaison Agency Inc., New York. **79**: No credit—AP/Wide World Photos. **80, 81**: Nik Wheeler/Black Star, New York; Francois Darquennes/Sygma, New York. **82, 83**: Photofest, New York; courtesy Antonio Alcalá. **84, 85**: Steve Schapiro/Black Star, New York, *People Weekly* © Time Inc. Reprinted with permission; Maurizio La Pira, Rome, *People Weekly* © Time Inc. Reprinted with permission; David Carradine from *People Weekly* © 1977 Julian Wasser. Reprinted with permission; Tony Costa, *People Weekly* © Time Inc. Reprinted with permission—photograph by Harry Benson, *People Weekly* © Time Inc. Reprinted with permission; Dale Wittner, *People Weekly* © Time Inc. Reprinted with permission; Steve Schapiro/Black Star, New York, *People Weekly* © Time Inc. Reprinted with permission; SUPERMAN: THE MOVIE © 1978 Film Export A.G. SUPERMAN is a registered trademark of DC Comics. *People Weekly* © Time Inc. Reprinted with permission—photograph by Harry Benson, *People Weekly* © Time Inc. Reprinted with permission; Stanley Tretick/Sygma, New York, *People Weekly* © Time Inc. Reprinted with permission; Betty Ford from *People Weekly* © 1978 Julian Wasser. Reprinted with permission. **86, 87**: Al Freni/*Life* Magazine; courtesy Antonio Alcalá; Globe Photos, New York; private collection; Al Freni/*Life* Magazine—Henry Groskinsky/*Life* Magazine (CB radio). **88**: Courtesy Jed Collectibles, Pemberton, N.J.; Michael Mauney/*Life* Magazine—Grey Villet/*Life* Magazine © Time Inc. **89**: Photograph by Harry Benson. **90**: Clothes courtesy Funk & Junk at http://www.funkandjunk.com (2)—© The New Yorker Collection 1970 Mischa Richter from cartoonbank.com. All rights reserved. **91**: Bill Ray/*Life* Magazine, © Time Inc. **92**: Henry Groskinsky/*Life* Magazine; photograph © 1998 Archives of Milton H. Greene, L.L.C., 541-997-4970, www.archivesmhg.com, *Life* Magazine © Time Inc. Reprinted with permission—no credit—John Stember/*Life* Magazine; SMP/Globe Photos, New York—© 1976 Newsweek Inc. All rights reserved. Reprinted by permission. Photograph by Francesco Scavullo courtesy Diane Von Furstenberg. **93**: Berry Berenson. **94**: Picture Press/Stern/Black Star, New York—Roxanne Lowit. **95**: Movie Still Archives, Harrison, Nebr. **96, 97**: John Olson/*Life* Magazine © Time Inc.; composite image: Nina Leen (woman), Lee Bolton courtesy Prado Museum, Madrid/*Life* Magazine © Time Inc. Reprinted with permission. **98, 99**: William Sievert, Rehoboth Beach, Del. (3); © Chicago Sun-Times, Chicago, Ill.—Bettye Lane, New York. **100**: William Sievert, Rehoboth Beach, Del.—Bettye Lane, New York. **101**: William Sievert, Rehoboth Beach, Del. (2 buttons); Sahm Doherty-Sefton, St. Michaels, Md.—private collection; Bettye Lane, New York. **102**: © 1970 Time Inc. Reprinted by permission; © 1972 Time Inc. Reprinted by permission; © 1976 Time Inc. Reprinted by permission—UPI/Corbis-Bettmann (2). **103**: © Ellen Shub, 1998, Newton, Mass.; William Sievert, Rehoboth Beach, Del. **104**: William Sievert, Rehoboth Beach, Del. (59¢)—UPI/Corbis-Bettmann; Bettye Lane, New York. **105**: © Earl Dotter, Silver Spring, Md. **106**: AP/Wide World Photos (3)—courtesy The International Tennis Hall of Fame & Museum, Newport, R.I. **107**: William Sievert, Rehoboth Beach, Del.; © 1978 Time Inc. Reprinted by permission—Bettye Lane, New York. **108, 109**: Alex Webb/Magnum Photos, Inc., New York; Smithsonian Institution, Washington, D.C. No. 79-7480. **110, 111**: © Barry Levine, courtesy Studio Chikara, Flushing, New York; Memory Shop, New York. **112**: Courtesy Ruth Goldberg, except *Playing Possum* courtesy Michael Ochs Archives, Venice, Calif., and *Hotel California* courtesy Kris Hanneman. **113**: © 1971 Joel Bernstein, Oakland, Calif. **114**: Courtesy The Bata Shoe Museum, Toronto, Ontario, Canada. **115**: Terry O'Neill, Camera Press, London. **116, 117**: Barry Plummer, Ascot, Berkshire, England. **118**: Michael

BIBLIOGRAPHY

BOOKS

African American Biography (Vol. 1, A-D). Detroit: Gale Research, 1994.

Allen, Woody. *Woody Allen on Woody Allen.* Ed. by Stig Björkman. New York: Grove Press, 1993.

The Almanac of American History. New York: G. P. Putnam's Sons, 1983.

Ambrose, Stephen. *Nixon* (Vol. 2). New York: Simon & Schuster, 1989.

American Decades: 1970-1979. Ed. by Victor Bondi. Detroit: Gale Research, 1995.

Anderson, Dave. *The Story of Basketball.* New York: Morrow, 1997.

Ball, Howard. *"We Have a Duty."* New York: Greenwood Press, 1990.

Barnard, Stephen. *Rock: An Illustrated History.* New York: Schirmer Books, 1986.

The Baseball Encyclopedia. New York: Macmillan, 1984.

Basinger, Jeanine. *American Cinema.* New York: Rizzoli, 1994.

Beck, J. Spencer (ed.). *The Variety History of Show Business.* New York: Harry N. Abrams, 1993.

Bernikow, Louise. *The American Women's Almanac.* New York: Berkley Books, 1997.

Bernstein, Carl, and Bob Woodward. *All the President's Men.* New York: Warner Books, 1974.

The Best of Sports Illustrated. New York: Sports Illustrated, 1996.

Bill, James A. *The Eagle and the Lion.* New Haven, Conn.: Yale University Press, 1988.

Blum, John Morton. *Years of Discord.* New York: W. W. Norton, 1991.

Bourne, Peter G. *Jimmy Carter.* New York: Scribner, 1997.

Bray, Howard. *The Pillars of the Post.* New York: W. W. Norton, 1980.

Brenner, Richard J. *The Complete Super Bowl Story: Games I-XXI.* New York: East End Publishing, 1987.

Carroll, Peter N. *It Seemed Like Nothing Happened: The Tragedy and Promise of America in the 1970s.* New York: Holt, Rinehart and Winston, 1982.

Carter, Jimmy. *Keeping Faith: Memoirs of a President.* New York: Bantam Books, 1982.

Castleman, Harry, and Walter J. Podrazik. *Watching TV.* New York: McGraw-Hill, 1982.

A Century of Women. Ed. by Alan Covey. Atlanta: TBS Books, 1994.

Chafe, William. *The Road to Equality.* New York: Oxford University Press, 1994.

Chronicle of the 20th Century. Mount Kisco, N.Y.: Chronicle Publications, 1987.

Cohen, Marcia. *The Sisterhood.* New York: Simon & Schuster, 1988.

Collins, Bud (ed.). *Bud Collins' Modern Encyclopedia of Tennis.* Detroit: Visible Ink Press, 1994.

Crothers, Tim. *Greatest Teams.* New York: Sports Illustrated, 1998.

Davidson, Bill. *Jane Fonda.* New York: Dutton, 1990.

DeBenedetti, Charles. *An American Ordeal.* Syracuse, N.Y.: Syracuse University Press, 1990.

The Decade of Women. Ed. by Suzanne Levine and Harriet Lyons. New York: G. P. Putnam's Sons, 1980.

Dougan, Clark, and Samuel Lipsman. *A Nation Divided* (The Vietnam Experience series). Boston: Boston Publishing Company, 1984.

Dougan, Clark, and Stephen Weiss. *The American Experience in Vietnam.* New York: W. W. Norton, 1988.

Edelstein, Andrew J., and Kevin McDonough. *The Seventies From Hot Pants to Hot Tubs.* New York: Dutton, 1990.

Edwards, John. *The Seventies.* London: Macdonald Educational, 1980.

Emery, Fred. *Watergate.* New York: Simon & Schuster, 1995.

Encyclopedia of the Vietnam War. Ed. by Stanley I. Kutler. New York: Macmillan, 1996.

Encyclopedia of World Biography (2nd ed.). Detroit: Gale, 1998.

Ervin, Sam J., Jr. *The Whole Truth.* New York: Random House, 1980.

Facts On File Yearbook: 1973. New York: Facts On File, 1974.

Fimrite, Ron. *The World Series.* Birmingham, Ala.: Oxmoor House, 1993.

Fitzgerald, Francis J. (ed.). *Greatest Moments in Pittsburgh Steelers History.* Louisville, Ky.: AdCraft, 1996.

Ford, Daniel F. *Three Mile Island.* New York: Penguin Books, 1982.

Garrett, Michael. *The Seventies.* Austin, Tex.: Steck-Vaughn, 1989.

Gordon, Lois G., and Alan Gordon. *American Chronicle.* New York: Atheneum, 1987.

Haden-Guest, Anthony. *The Last Party.* New York: Morrow, 1997.

Hamill, Dorothy. *Dorothy Hamill on and off the Ice.* New York: Alfred A. Knopf, 1983.

Hamilton, Sue L. *Days of Tragedy: The Death of a Cult Family.* Blooming-ton, Minn.: Abdo & Daughters, 1989.

Healey, Tim. *The 1970s.* London: Franklin Watts, 1989.

Hearst, Patricia Campbell. *Patty Hearst.* New York: Avon Books, 1988.

Heilbrun, Carolyn G. *The Education of a Woman: The Life of Gloria Steinem.* New York: Dial Press, 1995.

Hoobler, Dorothy, and Thomas Hoobler. *An Album of the Seventies.* New York: Franklin Watts, 1981.

Jarrett, William S. *Timetables of Sports History: Baseball.* New York: Facts On File, 1989.

Johnson, William Oscar. *The Olympics.* Birmingham, Ala.: Oxmoor House, 1992.

Kalinsky, George. *The New York Knicks.* New York: Macmillan, 1996.

Katz, Ephraim. *The Film Encyclopedia.* New York: Thomas Y. Crowell, 1979.

Keese, Parton. *The Measure of Greatness.* Englewood Cliffs, N.J.: Prentice-Hall, 1981.

Kissinger, Henry. *Diplomacy.* New York: Simon & Schuster, 1994.

Kleinfelder, Rita Lang. *When We Were Young.* New York: Prentice Hall, 1993.

Kutler, Stanley I. *The Wars of Watergate.* New York: Alfred A. Knopf, 1990.

Landau, Nathan. *Heavenly Deceptor.* [U.S.]: N. Landau, [1991].

Lax, Eric. *Woody Allen: A Biography.* New York: Alfred A. Knopf, 1991.

Lefcowitz, Eric. *The Rhino History of Rock 'n' Roll: The 70s.* New York: Pocket Books, 1997.

Lipsman, Samuel, and Stephen Weiss. *The False Peace* (The Vietnam Experience series). Boston: Boston Publishing Company, 1985.

McDaniel, Dorothy Howard. *After the Hero's Welcome.* Chicago: Bonus Books, 1991.

McLellan, Vin, and Paul Avery. *The Voices of Guns.* New York: G. P. Putnam's Sons, 1977.

McNeil, Alex. *Total Television* (4th ed.). New York: Penguin Books, 1996.

Magee, Michael. *Champions.* New York: Morrow, 1980.

Marc, David, and Robert J. Thompson. *Prime Time, Prime Movers.* Syracuse, N.Y.: Syracuse University Press, 1995.

Naipaul, Shiva. *Journey to Nowhere.* New York: Simon & Schuster, 1981.

Nelson, Polly. *Defending the Devil.* New York: Morrow, 1994.

The New Rolling Stone Encyclopedia of Rock and Roll. Ed. by Patricia Romanowski and Holly George-Warren. New York: Fireside, 1995.

Nicklaus, Jack. *Jack Nicklaus.* New York: Simon & Schuster, 1997.

Nixon, Richard M. *The Memoirs of Richard Nixon.* New York: Simon & Schuster, 1990.

Ochs, Michael. *1000 Record Covers.* London: Taschen, 1996.

The Official NBA Basketball Encyclopedia (2nd ed.). New York: Villard Books, 1994.

Osborne, Robert A. *65 Years of the Oscar.* New York: Abbeville Press, 1994.

Our Century: 1970-1980. Milwaukee: Gareth Stevens Publishing, 1993.

Our Glorious Century. Pleasantville, N.Y.: Reader's Digest, 1994.

Our Times. Atlanta: Turner Publishing, 1995.

Pacheco, Ferdie. *Muhammad Ali.* New York: Carol Publishing, 1992.

Palmer, Robert. *Rock and Roll.* New York: Harmony Books, 1995.

Patterson, James T. *Grand Expectations.* New York: Oxford University Press, 1996.

Peacock, John. *Fashion Sourcebooks: The 1970s.* London: Thames and Hudson, 1997.

Phillips, Louis, and Burnham Holmes. *The TV Almanac.* New York: Macmillan, 1994.

Pluto, Terry. *Loose Balls: The Short, Wild Life of the American Basketball Association.* New York: Simon & Schuster, 1990.

Pryor, Richard. *Pryor Convictions and Other Life Sentences.* New York: Pantheon Books, 1995.

Rees, Dafydd, and Luke Crampton. *Encyclopedia of Rock Stars.* New York: DK Publishing, 1996.

The Rolling Stone Illustrated History of Rock and Roll. Ed. by Jim Miller. New York: Random House, 1980.

Ryan, Mary P. *Womanhood in America.* New York: Franklin Watts, 1983.

Sackett, Susan. *The Hollywood Reporter Book of Box Office Hits.* New York: Billboard Books, 1996.

Safire, William. *Before the Fall.* Garden City, N.Y.: Doubleday, 1975.

Sheehan, Neil. *A Bright Shining Lie.* New York: Random House, 1988.

Smith, Desire. *Fashionable Clothing From the Sears Catalogs: Early 1970s.* Atglen, Pa.: Schiffer, 1998.

Steele, Valerie. *Fifty Years of Fashion.* New Haven, Conn.: Yale University Press, 1997.

Steinem, Gloria. *Outrageous Acts and Everyday Rebellions.* New York: Holt, Rinehart and Winston, 1983.

Stephens, Mark. *Three Mile Island.* New York: Random House, 1980.

The Story of Rock 'n' Roll. Miami, Fla.: Carlton, 1995.

Sullivan, George. *The Day the Women Got the Vote.* New York: Scholastic, 1994.

Taylor, L. B., Jr. *Hostage!* New York: Franklin Watts, 1989.

Tobler, John. *Elton John.* London: Hamlyn, 1995.

The Twentieth Century (Vol. 5). New York: Macmillan, 1992.

The Twentieth Century (Vol. 6). New York: Macmillan, 1992.

The Variety History of Show Business. New York: Harry N. Abrams, 1993.

Vaz, Mark Cotta. *Industrial Light and Magic.* New York: Ballantine Books, 1996.

Very Seventies. New York: Fireside, 1995.

Wallechinsky, David. *The Complete Book of the Olympics* (1992 ed.). Boston: Little, Brown, 1991.

War in the Shadows (The Vietnam Experience series). Boston: Boston Publishing Company, 1980.

Ward, Ed, Geoffrey Stokes, and Ken Tucker. *Rock of Ages.* New York: Summit Books, 1986.

Ward, Geoffrey C. *Baseball.* New York: Alfred A. Knopf, 1994.

Wells, Tim. *444 Days.* San Diego, Calif.: Harcourt Brace Jovanovich, 1985.

Whitburn, Joel. *Joel Whitburn's Top Pop: Singles 1955-1993.* Menomonee Falls, Wis.: Record Research, 1994.

Williams, John A., and Dennis A. Williams. *If I Stop I'll Die: The Comedy and Tragedy of Richard Pryor.* New York: Thunder's Mouth Press, 1991.

Winship, Michael. *Television.* New York: Random House, 1988.

Woodward, Bob, and Carl Bernstein. *The Final Days.* New York: Simon & Schuster, 1976.

Women in the 20th Century. New York: Time, 1997.

Wright, Robin B. *In the Name of God.* New York: Simon & Schuster, 1989.

Young, Marilyn B. *The Vietnam Wars: 1945-1990.* New York: Harper-Collins, 1991.

PERIODICALS

"A Celebration of One Hundred Years." *New York Times Magazine,* April 14, 1996.

Lemann, Nicholas. "How the Seventies Changed America." *American Heritage,* July/August 1991.

Lewis, Alfred E. "Five Held in Plot to Bug Democrats' Office Here." *Washington Post,* June 18, 1972.

Life, January 1970-December 1972; January-December 1979.

Life, Special Issues, 1973-1978.

Lucas, John A. Letter to the editor. *Wall Street Journal,* August 6, 1998.

People, March 1974-December 1979.

Time, January 1970-December 1979.

Webb, James. "The Media's War on Vietnam Vets" (op-ed piece). *Wall Street Journal,* July 15, 1998.

Vachon, Brian. "The Jesus Movement Is Upon Us." *Look,* February 9, 1971.

Washington Post, January 1972-December 1974.

Wolfe, Tom. "The 'Me' Decade and the Third Great Awakening." *New York,* August 23, 1976.

INDEX

A

Aaron, Hank, *156; timeline* 27; quoted, 156
ABC News Nightline (TV show), 174
Abdul-Jabbar, Kareem, *160*
Abortion, legalization of, 28, 44, *100, 101; timeline* 26
Abzug, Bella, *108-109;* quoted, 109
Academy Awards, 40, 42, 86, 176, 180, 181, 182; *timeline* 23, 25, 26, 27, 29, 31, 33
Affirmative action, 26-28
Afghanistan, *timeline* 33
AFL-CIO, 26
Agnew, Spiro T., 6, *54-55; timeline* 27; resignation of, 22, 32, 64; quoted, 55
Aircraft, *timeline* 29. See also Skyjackings
Alda, Alan, 172, *173*
Ali, Muhammad, 6, 91, *165; timeline* 27, 29, 32; quoted, 164
Alien (movie), *184*
Allen, Paul, *timeline* 29
Allen, Woody, 34, *43;* quoted, 42, 43
All in the Family (TV show), 170, *171*
Allman Brothers (music group), *126*
All the President's Men (movie), *180*
All Things Considered (radio show), *timeline* 23
American Bicentennial, *8-9,* 22; *timeline* 30
American Graffiti (movie), 178
American Indian Movement, *timeline* 27
Amin, Hafizullah, *timeline* 33
Amoco Cadiz oil spill, *12-13*
Annie Hall (movie), 6, 42, *92*
Antiwar movement, 40, *70-71, 72,* 74
Apocalypse Now (movie), *185*
Apollo space missions, *20-21; timeline* 29
Apple Computer Inc., *timeline* 29
Ashe, Arthur, *166*
Atlanta Braves, *timeline* 27
Attica State Correctional Facility riot, *132-133; timeline* 24
Autobiography of Howard Hughes, The (Irving), *timeline* 25
Autobiography of Malcom X, The, 48
Aykroyd, Dan, *175*

B

Baker, Howard, *62-63;* quoted, 62
Banks, Dennis, *timeline* 27
Bannister, Roger, 164
Barker, Bernard, *56*
Baryshnikov, Mikhail, *timeline* 27
Beatles, the (music group), 125
Bee Gees (music group), *122*
Begin, Menachem, *timeline* 32
Belushi, John, *175*
Bench, Johnny, *158*
Benchley, Peter, 178

Benny, Jack, 34
Bernstein, Carl, *58,* 59, 180
Bicentennial (U.S.), *8-9,* 22; *timeline* 30
Bionic Woman, The (TV show), 174
Black Americans. *See* Civil rights; Racial issues; *specific persons*
Blaxploitation movies, *184*
Blazing Saddles (movie), 38, *185*
Blondie (music group), 128
Books, 26; *timeline 23,* 25, 26, 27, 28, 29, 31, 33; *Roots: The Saga of an American Family,* 28, 48; on self-improvement, *148, 151, 153;* on sex, *88;* on women's rights, 97, *101, 103*
Borg, Bjorn, *timeline* 31
Bork, Robert, 65
Boston Celtics, 160
Bowie, David, 126, *127*
Boxing, *165; timeline* 27, 29, 32
Bradshaw, Terry, *162*
Brando, Marlon, *176-177,* 180
Brezhnev, Leonid, *53*
Brooks, Mel, 38
Brown, James, quoted, 118
Brown, Louise, *timeline* 31
Browne, Jackson, 112
Brownmiller, Susan, 102, 103
Bundy, Theodore Robert, *136-137;* quoted, 137
Burnett, Carol, *170*
Business and industry: *timeline* 29; employment, 26-28, *104-105. See also* Products, new
Butterfield, Alexander, quoted, 63

C

Cabaret (movie), *182*
Calley, William, 72; *timeline* 23
Cambodia: *timeline 32;* and Vietnam War, 22, 68, 70-72, 80
Camp David accords, 32; *timeline* 32
Capote, Truman, 94
Carol Burnett Show (TV show), *170*
Carpenters (music group), *111*
Carson, Johnny, *35;* quoted, 34, 35
Carter, Billy, 86
Carter, Jimmy, 34, *46-47,* 86, *102; timeline* 31, *32;* and Hearst case, 139; and Iran hostage crisis, 32, 46, 142; and public opinion, 32, 46; quoted, 32, 46, 47
Carter, John Mack, 102
Carter, Judy, quoted, 109
Carter, "Miss Lillian," quoted, 94
Carter, Lynda, *174*
Carter, Rosalynn, *46-47, 108-109*
Cavett, Dick, *6;* quoted, 6
Central Intelligence Agency, 24, 56, 59, 67
Cernan, Gene, 20
Chamberlain, Wilt, *160*
Charlie's Angels (TV show), *168*-170, 174
Chase, Chevy, quoted, 174
Chico and the Man (TV show), 170-172
China: *timeline* 25, 33; and Nixon

administration, *36-37, 52,* 76
Chinatown (movie), *182*
Chorus Line, A (musical), *timeline* 29
Chou En-lai, *52*
Christgau, Robert, quoted, 114
Church of Scientology, 154
Cincinnati Reds, 158, *159*
Cisler, Lucinda, quoted, 100
Civil rights, *10-11,* 28, *98-99; timeline 23,* 25. *See also* Legal issues; Racial issues
Cleland, Max, 46
Cleveland Browns, *timeline* 23
Clinton, George, *120-121;* quoted, 121
Clockwork Orange (movie), *185*
Columbo (TV show), *timeline* 24
Comaneci, Nadia, *timeline* 30
Comfort, Alex, 88
Coming Home (movie), 40, *182*
Communism, 22; and Nixon, *52. See also* Vietnam War
Complete Book of Running, The (Fixx), *151*
Concorde airliner, *timeline* 29
Connors, Jimmy, *166; timeline* 31
Cooper, D. B., *timeline* 24
Coppola, Francis Ford, 176-178
Cosby, Bill, quoted, 38
Cosell, Howard, *timeline* 23
Costello, Elvis, 128
Cox, Archibald, 59, 64, *65; timeline* 27
Cox, Edward, 66; *timeline* 23
Cox, Tricia Nixon, *66-67; timeline* 23
Crime: *timeline 23,* 24, 27, 29, 32; Bundy case, *136-137;* Hearst case, *138-139;* Jonestown incident, 6, 32, *140-141;* prison riot, *132-133;* skyjackings, 6, *134-135;* against women, 100, *101. See also* Terrorism
Curtin, Jane, *175*

D

Dash, Samuel, *62-63*
Davis, Adele, 153
Davis, Angela, *timeline* 23
Dayan, Moshe, 94
Dean, Elton, 114
Dean, John, 59, *60-61,* 63
Deliverance (movie), *184-185*
Democratic National Committee headquarters, 24, 25, *56-57*
De Niro, Robert, 180
Derek, Bo, *82*
Derek and the Dominos (music group), *126*
Disco, *14-15,* 94, 95, *122, 123*
Divine Light Mission, 154
Doonesbury (comic strip), *timeline* 23
Drug use, 94, 111; *timeline* 22, 24, 31
Dunaway, Faye, *182*
Dylan, Bob, 125

E

Eagles, the (music group), 112
Earth, Wind and Fire (music group), 121

Earth Day, *timeline* 22
Earthquake (movie), *184*
Eastwood, Clint, *180*
Economic issues: *timeline 33;* recession, 22, 24-26, 32; unemployment, *16-17*
Egypt: *timeline* 31, 32; peace negotiations with Israel, 32
Ehrlichman, John, 52, 59, 62, *63;* quoted, 63
Eisenhower, Dwight D., 51
Ellsberg, Daniel, 54, 62
Energy crisis, 22, 24-26, 32, 33; *timeline 27,* 33
Environmental issues, *12-13,* 30, *144-145; timeline* 22, 23, 31, 33
Environmental Protection Agency, 30, 52; *timeline* 23
Equal Rights Amendment (1972), *98-99; timeline* 25
Erhard, Werner, 30, 148
Ervin, Sam J., Jr., *62-63,* 64; quoted, 60
Erving, Julius ("Dr. J."), 160, *161*
Esalen Institute, *148, 149*
Esquire, 44
Est (Erhard Seminar Training), 30, 148
Evert, Chris, *166; timeline* 31
Exorcist, The (movie), *185*

F

Falwell, Jerry, *timeline* 33
Farenthold, Frances ("Sissy"), 45
Farrow, Mia, *84*
Fashions: and music, *114, 115, 124, 125*-126; trends, 86, *87, 90-93, 94, 151*
Fat Albert and the Cosby Kids (TV show), *timeline* 25
Fawcett-Majors, Farrah, *168*
FBI (Federal Bureau of Investigation), 24, 54, 134, 139; and Watergate, 56, 59, 67
Feminine Mystique, The (Friedan), 97
Field, Sally, *182;* quoted, 182
Finley, Charlie, 158
Fischer, Bobby, 6; *timeline* 25
Fisher, Carrie, *178*
Fixx, Jim, quoted, 151
Fleetwood Mac (music group), *112*
Fonda, Jane, 6, 34, *40-41, 182; timeline* 25; quoted, 40
Foods: fads, 86, *87;* health foods, 147, *152, 153*
Ford, Betty, *108-109; timeline* 28
Ford, Gerald R., 36, *85; timeline 27, 28, 29,* 31; and public opinion, 32; as vice president, 64; quoted, 22, 32, 67
Ford, Harrison, *178*
Foreman, George, *165; timeline* 27
Foyt, A. J., *timeline* 31
Frampton, Peter, *timeline* 31
Frazier, Joe, 6; *timeline* 29
Frazier, Walt, *160*
Friedan, Betty, quoted, 97, 98
Fromme, Lynette ("Squeaky"), *time-*

line 29
Furstenberg, Diane von, *92*

G

Garfunkel, Art, 112
Gates, Bill, *timeline 29*
Gaye, Marvin, *118;* quoted, 118
Gay rights, 28-30, *88*
Godfather, The (movie), *176-177,* 178, 180
Gonzales, Virgilio, *56*
Good Times (TV show), 170
Gray, L. Patrick, 59
Grease (movie), *185*
Green, Al, *118*
Greene, "Mean Joe", *163;* quoted, 162

H

Haas, William, 134
Haig, Alexander M., *77*
Haldeman, H. R. (Bob), 52-54, 59, 62, *63,* 65
Haley, Alex, 28, 34, *49, 168;* quoted, 48
Halston (designer), *14-15*
Hamill, Dorothy, *164; timeline 29*
Hamill, Mark, *178*
"Hanoi Hilton," *78*
Happy Days (TV show), *timeline 28*
Harris, Franco, *162*
Harris, Thomas A., 148
Hart, Gary, quoted, 144
Health foods, 147, *152, 153*
Hearst, Patricia, *138-139; timeline 27;* quoted, 139
Hellman, Lillian, quoted, 97
Hendrix, Jimi, 6, 111; *timeline 22*
Henson, Jim, 170
Hijackings, 6, *134-135; timeline 23,* 24
Hoffa, Jimmy, *timeline 29*
Hoffman, Dustin, *180*
Hogan, Ben, 164
Holiday, Billie, 38
Hoover, J. Edgar, 54
Hubbard, L. Ron, 154
Hughes, Howard, 6; *timeline 25*
"Human potential" movement, 147, 148
Hunt, E. Howard, 56, 58, *59*

I

Incredible Hulk, The (TV show), *timeline 33*
International Society for Krishna Consciousness, *154*
Iran, shah of, 142
Iran hostage crisis, 32, 46, *142-143,* 174; *timeline 33*
Irving, Clifford, *timeline 25*
Israel: *timeline 25,* 32; peace negotiations with Egypt, 32; and terrorism, 131; Yom Kippur War, 26, 36

J

Jackson, Kate, *168*
Jackson, Keith, *timeline 23*
Jackson, Michael, *116-117*
Jackson, Reggie, *158;* quoted, 158
Jackson 5 (music group), 116

Jackson State University (Mississippi), 22, 70; *timeline 22*
Jagger, Bianca, *14-15*
Jagger, Mick, *124, 128;* quoted, 125
Jaworski, Leon, 65
Jaws (movie), *176,* 178
Jefferson, Thomas, 46
Jeffersons, The (TV show), 170
Jenner, Bruce, *166*
Jesus freaks, 154, *155*
Jobs, Steve, *timeline 29*
John, Elton, 114, *115;* quoted, 114
John Paul II, *84-85; timeline 33*
Johnson, Earl, *75*
Johnson, Lady Bird, *108-109*
Johnson, Lyndon Baines, 51, 65
Jones, Bobby, 164
Jones, Jim, 32, *140; timeline 32*
Jonestown mass suicide, 6, 32, *140-141; timeline 32*
Joplin, Janis, 6; *timeline 22*
Joy of Sex, The (Comfort), *88*

K

Katzen, Mollie, *153*
Keaton, Diane, *92*
Kennedy, Edward, quoted, 80
Kennedy, Florynce, quoted, 101
Kennedy, John F., 51, 65
Kennedy Center for the Performing Arts, *timeline 24*
Kent State University (Ohio), 22, *70-71; timeline 22*
Khmer Rouge, 22, 80; *timeline 32*
Khomeini, Ruhollah, *142-143*
Khrushchev, Nikita, 53
King, Billie Jean, 6, *106,* 107; *timeline 27*
King, Martin Luther, Jr., 24, 42
Kiss (music group), *110-111*
Kissinger, Henry, *36-37; timeline 26;* and foreign policy, 34, 36, 72, 76, *77;* quoted, 36, 77
Kleindienst, Richard, 59
Klute (movie), 40, *182*
Kojak (TV show), *174*
Kool and the Gang (music group), 121
Koppel, Ted, 174

L

Labor. *See* Business and industry
Ladies' Home Journal, 44, 102
Lady Sings the Blues (movie), 38
Lambert, Jack, *163*
Law, Tom, *146-147*
Lear, Norman, 170
Le Duc Tho, 76; *timeline 26;* quoted, 72
Led Zeppelin (music group), *125,* 126
Legal issues: *timeline 24, 26, 27;* abortion, 28, 44, *100, 101;* affirmative action, 26-28; environmental legislation, 30. *See also* Civil rights; U.S. Congress; Women's rights
Let's Eat Right to Keep Fit (Davis), 153
Liddy, G. Gordon, 56, *59*
Life magazine, 6, *69, 89, 92,* 97; *timeline 23, 25*

Little House on the Prairie (TV show), 174
Los Angeles Dodgers, *timeline 27*
Los Angeles Times, 114
Love Canal pollution, *timeline 31*
Lovell, James, quoted, 104
Love Story (Segal), *timeline 23*
Lucas, George, 176, 178; quoted, 178

M

McCord, James, *56,* 59
McCorvey, Norma, 100
McGovern, George, 54, 59; *timeline 25*
McLaren, Malcolm, 128
MacNeil, Tara, *103*
Magazines, *timeline 26,* 28. *See also specific publications*
Maginnes, Nancy, 36
Magruder, Jeb Stuart, 59
Maharishi Mahesh Yogi, 148
Majors, Lee, 174
Malcolm X, 48
Mao Zedong, 52; *timeline 24*
Mars exploration, *timeline 31*
Martinez, Eugenio, *56*
Mary Tyler Moore Show, The (TV show), 170, *172*
*M*A*S*H** (TV show), 172, *173*
Maude (TV show), 170
Means, Russell, *timeline 27*
Mean Streets (movie), 178
Me Decade. *See* Self-improvement movement
Medical developments, 6; *timeline 23,* 30, *31;* AHA statement on alcohol, 30; APA classifications, 28-30; health foods, 147, *152, 153;* and women's rights, 101
Meditation, 30, 147, *148*
Meredith, Don, *timeline 23*
Meyner, Helen, quoted, 107
Miami Dolphins, *162; timeline 26*
Microsoft, *timeline 29*
Mike Douglas Show, The (TV show), 38
Miller, Jeffrey Glenn, *70*
Millett, Kate, *102,* 103
Minnelli, Liza, *14-15,* 94, *182*
Mitchell, John, 59, *62;* quoted, 62
Mitchell, Joni, 112
Monday Night Football (TV show), *timeline 23*
Moon, Sun Myung, 154
Moon landing (1972), *20-21*
Moore, Mary Tyler, 6, 170, *172*
Moore, Sara Jane, *timeline 29*
Moosewood Cookbook (Katzen), *153*
"Moral Disarmament of Betty Coed, The" (Steinem), 44
Morgan, Joe, *158*
Morgan, Robin, *101,* 103
Morrison, Jim, 128; *timeline 24*
Motown music, *116-118*
Movies, *176-185;* directors, 42, *43, 176-179;* posters, *184-185;* stars, 38, *39, 40-41, 180-181;* women in, *82, 92, 182-183*
Ms. magazine, 44, *102,* 103; 109

Mueller, Peter, *timeline 29*
Muppet Show, The (TV show), *170*
Music, *110-129; timeline 22, 24, 31;* black, *116-121;* disco, 94, 95, *122, 123;* funk, *120-*121; in movies, 42; punk, *128, 129;* rock and roll, *110-111, 112, 113,* 114, *115, 124-127*
Muskie, Edmund, 54, *55*
My Lai massacre, 72; *timeline 23*

N

National Organization for Women, 97
National Public Radio, *timeline 23*
National Women's Conference, *108-109; timeline 31*
Network (movie), 182
Newman, Laraine, *175*
Newman, Randy, 112
New York City: and Bicentennial (U.S.), *8-9,* 22; protesters in, *96-97, 101, 104. See also specific locations and organizations*
New York Jets, *timeline 23*
New York Knicks, *160*
New York magazine, 44, *147*
New York Nets, 160, *161*
New York Times, 65, 72; *timeline 23*
New York Yankees, *158*
Nguyen Van Thieu, 69; quoted, 80
Nicholson, Jack, *180*
Nicklaus, Jack, *164*
Niven, David, 86
Nixon, Pat, *52,* 66-67
Nixon, Richard M., 36, *51-67; timeline 22, 25, 27,* 28; achievements of, 51-52; campaigning, *50-51,* 54–55; and foreign policy, 36, *52, 53;* quoted, 52, 54, 59, 64, 65, 69, 70-72, 76, 80; resignation of, 6, 22, 24, 32, *66-67;* and Vietnam War, 22-24, 40, *52,* 54, 69-72, 80; and Watergate, 54, 56-59, 61-63, *64,* 65
Nixon, Tricia. *See* Cox, Tricia Nixon
Nobel Peace Prize, 36; *timeline 33*
Noll, Chuck, quoted, 162
Norma Rae (movie), *182*
Nuclear power, *144-145; timeline 33*
Nyro, Laura, 112

O

Oakland Athletics, 158
Oakland Raiders, *162-163*
O'Brien, Lawrence, 56
O'Connor, Carroll, *171*
Oil embargo, 22, 24-26, 32; *timeline 27*
On Broadway Tonight (TV show), 38
One Flew Over the Cuckoo's Nest (movie), *180*
Oswald, Russell, 132
Our Bodies, Ourselves (Boston Women's Health Book Collective), *101*

P

Pacino, Al, *180*
Page, Jimmy, *125,* 126
Palestine: *timeline 23, 25;* and terrorism, 131

Palmer, Arnold, 164
Palmer, Jim, *158*
Parliament/Funkadelic (music group), *120-121*
Patton (movie), *184-185*
Pauling, Linus, *153; timeline* 23
Pentagon Papers, 54, 72; *timeline* 23
People magazine, *84-85;* quoted, 39
Physical fitness movement, 30, 83, 147, *150-151*
Pink Floyd (music group), 126
Pittsburgh Steelers, *162-163*
Playboy Club, 44
Politics, 24, *45; timeline* 33; on TV, 170, 171. *See also specific organizations and persons*
Presley, Elvis, 6; *timeline* 31
Prine, John, 112
Prison riots, *132-133; timeline* 24
Products, new, *timeline* 23, 25, 26, 27, 28, 29, 31, 33
Pryor, Richard, 34, *39;* quoted, 38, 39
Punk rock music, *128, 129*
Puzo, Mario, 178

Q

Queen (music group), *126*

R

Racial issues: *timeline 23,* 29; and Attica riot, *132-133;* interracial relationships, *88;* progress in, *10-11,* 26-28; and TV, 28, 48, *168-169,* 170-172
Radner, Gilda, *175*
Ramones, the (music group), *128*
Reagan, Ronald, election of, 32, 142
Redford, Robert, *180,* 183
Reiner, Rob, *171*
Religion: *timeline 32, 33;* Jonestown, 6, 32, *140-141;* and self-improvement, 30-32, 83, 147, *154, 155*
Richards, Keith, 128
Richards, Renee, *timeline* 30
Richardson, Elliot, 59, 65
Riggs, Bobby, 107; *timeline* 27
Risner, Robinson, *78*
Ritter, John, 174
Rockefeller, Nelson, 132
Rocky (movie), *181*
Roe v. Wade, 28, 100; *timeline* 26
Rolling Stone magazine, *123*
Rolling Stones, the (music group), *119, 124,* 125-126
Ronson, Mick, *127*
Ronstadt, Linda, *112*
Roots (Haley), 28, 48
Roots (TV show), 28, 48, *168-169*
Rose, Pete, *159;* quoted, 158
Roszak, Theodore, quoted, 154
Ruckelshaus, William, 65
Ryan, Leo, 140
Ryan, Nolan, *158*

S

Sadat, Anwar el-, *timeline 32*
St. John, Jill, 36
Sanford and Son (TV show), 170, *172*
Saturday Night Fever (movie), *95,* 122

Saturday Night Live (TV show), 38, 174, *175*
Savalas, Telly, *174*
Schlafly, Phyllis, 98, *99*
Schmidt, Mike, *158*
Schmitt, Jack, *20-21*
Scorsese, Martin, 176, 178
Scranton, William, 70
Secretariat (horse), *167; timeline* 26
Segal, Erich, *timeline* 23
Self-improvement movement, *146-155;* emotions, 30, 83, *146-147, 148, 149;* health foods, 147, *152, 153;* Me Decade, 30, 147; physical fitness, 30, 83, 147, *150-151;* and religion, 30-32, 83, 147, *154, 155*
Serpico (movie), *180*
Sex Pistols, the (music group), 128, *129*
Sexual Politics (Millett), 103
Sexual relationships, *88, 89*
Shaft (movie), *184-185*
Shampoo (movie), *184-185*
Shriver, Pam, *timeline* 31
Simon, Carly, 112
Simon, Paul, *112*
Sirica, John J., *57,* 64-65; quoted, 59
Six Million Dollar Man, The (TV show), *174*
Skyjackings, 6, *134-135; timeline* 23, 24
Slang, '70s slang, *table* 87
Sleeper (movie), 42
Smith, Jaclyn, *168*
Smith, Patti, *128;* quoted, 128
Snead, Sam, 164
Somers, Suzanne, 174
South Africa, *timeline* 29
Soviet Union: *timeline* 25, 29, 33; and Nixon, 36, 52, 53, 70, 76
Space age, *20-21; timeline 29, 31,* 33
Spassky, Boris, *timeline* 25
Spielberg, Steven, 178; quoted, 176
Spinks, Leon, *timeline* 32
Spitz, Mark, 6, *156-157; timeline 25;* quoted, 156
Sports, *156-167; timeline* 23, 25, 26, 27, 29, *30,* 31, 32; baseball, *107, 156, 158-159;* basketball, *160-161;* fitness, 30, 83, 147, *150-151;* football, *162-163;* heroes of, *164-167;* Olympic Games, *131-132, 156-157, 164, 166;* and women's rights, 106-107
Sports Illustrated, 156, 160, 162, 164, 166; quoted, 158
"Stairway to Heaven" (song), 126
Stallone, Sylvester, 180, *181*
Stapleton, Jean, *171*
Star Wars (movie), 178, *179*
Steinem, Gloria, 34, *45, 102,* 103; quoted, 44, 102, 104
Stirm, Robert, *79*
Stone, Sly, 118-*121*
Stratton, Richard, quoted, 79
Streaking, *86-87*
Streisand, Barbra, *183*
Struthers, Sally, *171*
Students: *timeline* 22; coed dorms,

88; protests by, 22, *70-71*
Studio 54 (disco), *14-15,* 94, 122
Sturgis, Frank, 56
Summer, Donna, *122*
Super Bowl, *162-163; timeline* 26
Supreme Court: *timeline* 23, 26; and abortion rights, 28, 100; and Watergate, 65, 67
Swann, Lynn, 162
Switzer, Katherine, 106
Symbionese Liberation Army, 139; *timeline* 27

T

Taiwan, *timeline* 33
Talking Heads (music group), 128
Taupin, Bernie, 114
Taxi (TV show), *172*
Taxi Driver (movie), 176, 178, 180
Taylor, James, *112*
Television, *168-175; timeline* 23, 24, 25, 27, 28, 29, 31, *33;* personalities, 34, *35,* 38, *39;* program topics, *168-175; Roots,* 28, 48, *168-169;* sports programs, 107, 160, 164; and Vietnam War, 70, 172; and Watergate, 61-62, *64,* 65, 170
Television (music group), 128
10 (movie), *82*
Teresa, Mother, *timeline* 33
Terrorism, 32, 46, *131-132, 142-143,* 174; *timeline* 23, 25, *33. See also* Crime
That Nigger's Crazy (album), 38
There's a Riot Goin' On (album), *121*
Thomas, Marlo, 36
Three Mile Island accident, *144-145; timeline* 33
Three's Company (TV show), 174
Time magazine, *52, 102, 107, 167, 168; timeline 23, 27,* 30; quoted, 60
Tomlin, Lily, 38
Tonight Show, The (TV show), 34
Transactional analysis, *148*
Trans-Alaska Pipeline, *timeline* 31
Travolta, John, *95*
Treasures of Tutankhamen exhibit, *timeline* 31
Trudeau, Garry, *timeline* 23
Turcotte, Ron, *167*

U

Unification Church, *154*
U.S. Bicentennial, *8-9,* 22; *timeline* 30
U.S. Congress: *timeline* 23, 25, 27; hearings on CIA, 24; and Vietnam War, 80; and Watergate, *60-63,* 65, 67. *See also* Legal issues
U.S. presidential elections, 54; *timeline* 25, 31

V

Vallee, Rudy, 38
Van Gelder, Lindsy, quoted, 109
Vicious, Sid, *129*
Vietnam Veterans Against the War, 72
Vietnam War, *68-81; timeline* 22, *23,* 25, 26, 29, 31; antiwar movement, 40, *70-71,* 72, *74;* casualties of, 24,

88; protests by, 22, *70-71*

69, 74, *75, 76, 81;* end of, *80, 81;* escalation of, 22, 69; history of, 22-24, 70; impact of, 6; and Nixon, 22-24, 40, *52,* 54, 69-72, 80; peace negotiations, 24, 36, 76, *77;* POWs, 24, 76, *78, 79,* 80; and public opinion, 22-24, 69-72, *74,* 76; Saigon evacuation, *6-7,* 24, *80;* troop withdrawals, 24, 69, 70, 72, 80; and TV, 70, 172; U.S. air power, *73,* 74
Viking space mission, *timeline 31*
Village People (music group), 122, *123*
Vitamin C, the Common Cold, and the Flu (Pauling), 153
Voting rights, *timeline* 24

W

Wagner, Lindsay, 174
Wainwright, Loudon, III, 112
Waits, Tom, 112
Wallace, Cornelia, *timeline* 25
Wallace, George, *timeline* 25
Waltons, The (TV show), *172*
War (music group), 116
Warhol, Andy, *14-15,* 94
Washington Bullets, 160
Washington Post, 58, 59, 180
Washington Redskins, *timeline* 26
Waskow, Thomas, *74*
Watergate scandal, *50-67; timeline* 25, *27;* break-in, 24, *56-59;* hearings, *60-63,* 65, 67; impact of, 6, 46; movie, *180;* "Plumbers" formed, 54; and public opinion, 24, 62, 65, 67; resolution of, *66-67;* tapes, 63, 64-65, 67; and TV, 61-62, *64,* 65, 170
Way We Were, The (movie), *183*
Wills, Frank, 56
Wolfe, Tom, 30; quoted, 147, 148, 154
Women: fashions for, *92, 93, 94;* in movies, *82, 92, 182-183. See also specific persons*
Women's rights, *96-109; timeline* 29, 31; and abortion, 28, 44, *100, 101;* and employment, 28, *104-105;* and legislation, 98- *99,* 107, 109; and movies, 182; National Women's Conference, *108-109;* origins of, 28, 97; and publishing, *97, 101, 102-103;* and sports, *106-107;* and TV, 168-170; and violence, 100, *101*
Women's Strike for Equality, *96-97*
Wonder, Stevie, 118, *119*
Wonder Woman (TV show), *174*
Woods, Rose Mary, 65
Woodward, Bob, 58, 59, 180
World Series, 158, *159*
Wozniak, Steve, *timeline* 29

Y

Yoga, *146-147*
Yom Kippur War, 26, 36
Young, Neil, 112, *113*
Young, Sheila, *timeline* 29

Z

Ziegler, Ron, quoted, 59
Ziggy Stardust show, 126, *127*

Time-Life Books is a division of Time Life Inc.

TIME LIFE INC.
PRESIDENT and CEO: George Artandi

TIME-LIFE BOOKS

PUBLISHER/MANAGING EDITOR: Neil Kagan
VICE PRESIDENT, MARKETING: Joseph A. Kuna

OUR AMERICAN CENTURY
Time of Transition: The 70s

EDITORS: Loretta Britten, Paul Mathless
DIRECTOR, NEW PRODUCT DEVELOPMENT:
Elizabeth D. Ward
DIRECTOR OF MARKETING: Pamela R. Farrell

Deputy Editor: Kristin Hanneman
Associate Editor/Research and Writing: Anastasia Warpinski
Assistant Product Manager: Terri Miller
Picture Associate: Anne Whittle
Senior Copyeditor: Anne Farr
Technical Art Specialist: John Drummond
Picture Coordinator: Betty H. Weatherley
Editorial Assistant: Christine Higgins

Design for **Our American Century** by Antonio Alcalá,
Studio A, Alexandria, Virginia.

Special Contributors: Janet Cave, Alexis Doster III, Lee Hassig,
Diana Morgan, Robert Speziale (writing and editing); Ronald
H. Bailey, George Daniels, Jerry Dunn, Robert Hull, Darcie
Conner Johnston, Alison Kahn, John Newton, Ellen Phillips
(writing); Mimi Harrison, Jennifer Veech (research and writ-
ing); Patti Cass, Ruth Goldberg, Jessica Jacob, Susan V. Kelly,
Daniel Kulpinski, Jane Martin, Marilyn Terrell (research);
Kimberly Grandcolas (production); Richard Friend,
Marti Davila (design); Susan Nedrow (index).

Correspondents: Maria Vincenza Aloisi (Paris); Christine Hinze
(London), Christina Lieberman (New York).

Director of Finance: Christopher Hearing
Directors of Book Production: Marjann Caldwell, Patricia Pascale
Director of Publishing Technology: Betsi McGrath
Director of Photography and Research: John Conrad Weiser
Director of Editorial Administration: Barbara Levitt
Production Manager: Gertraude Schaefer
Quality Assurance Manager: James King
Chief Librarian: Louise D. Forstall

EDITORIAL CONSULTANT
Richard B. Stolley is currently senior editorial adviser at Time
Inc. After 19 years at *Life* magazine as a reporter, bureau chief,
and assistant managing editor, he became the first managing
editor of *People* magazine, a position he held with great success
for eight years. He then returned to *Life* magazine as managing
editor and later served as editorial director for all Time Inc.
magazines. In 1997 Stolley received the Henry Johnson Fisher
Award for Lifetime Achievement, the magazine industry's high-
est honor.

Library of Congress Cataloging-in-Publication Data
Time of transition : the 70s / by the editors of Time-Life Books ;
with a foreword by Dick Cavett.
p. cm.—(Our American century)
Includes bibliographical references (p.) and index.
ISBN 0-7835-5507-5
1. United States—History—1969- 2. United States—History—
1969—Pictorial works. 3. Nineteen seventies. 4. Nineteen
seventies—Pictorial works.
I. Time-Life Books. II. Series.
E839.T54 1998
973.924—dc21   98-38957
                                                        CIP

Other History Publications:

What Life Was Like
The American Story
Voices of the Civil War
The American Indians
Lost Civilizations
Mysteries of the Unknown
Time Frame
The Civil War
Cultural Atlas

For information on and a full description of any of the
Time-Life Books series listed above,
please call 1-800-621-7026
or write:

Reader Information
Time-Life Customer Service
P.O. Box C-32068
Richmond, Virginia 23261-2068